100 GREATS SHEFFIELD UNITED FOOTBALL CLUB

The United players of 1948/49.

100 GREATS

SHEFFIELD UNITED
FOOTBALL CLUB

WRITTEN BY
DENIS CLAREBROUGH

TEMPUS

First published 2001, reprinted 2003
Copyright © Denis Clarebrough, 2001

Tempus Publishing Limited
The Mill, Brimscombe Port,
Stroud, Gloucestershire, GL5 2QG

ISBN 0 7524 2264 2

Typesetting and origination by
Tempus Publishing Limited
Printed in Great Britain by
Midway Colour Print, Wiltshire

Present and forthcoming football titles from Tempus Publishing:

Another Day at the Office (Roger Freestone)	Pb 128pp	Keith Haynes	0 7524 2167 9	£12.99
Cambridge United FC	Images	Attmore & Nurse	0 7524 2256 1	£9.99
Charlton Athletic FC	Images	David Ramzan	0 7524 1504 2	£9.99
Crystal Palace FC	Greats	Revd Nigel Sands	0 7524 2176 X	£12.00
Everton FC 1880-1946	Images	John Rowlands	0 7524 2259 6	£10.99
Forever England	Pb 192pp	Mark Shaoul	0 7524 2042 9	£17.99
Gillingham FC	Images	Roger Triggs	0 7524 1567 0	£9.99
Gillingham FC	Players	Roger Triggs	0 7524 2243 X	£17.99
Ipswich Town FC	Images	Tony Garnett	0 7524 2152 2	£9.99
Leeds United FC	Images	David Saffer	0 7524 1642 1	£9.99
Leeds United in Europe	Images	David Saffer	0 7524 2043 7	£9.99
Leyton Orient FC	Images	Neilson Kaufman	0 7524 2094 1	£10.99
Manchester City FC	Classics	David Saffer	0 7524 2255 3	£12.00
Millwall FC 1885-1939	Images	Millwall FC Museum	0 7524 1849 1	£9.99
Queens Park Rangers FC	Images	Tony Williamson	0 7524 1604 9	£9.99
Reading FC	Greats	David Downs	0 7524 2081 X	£9.99
Reading FC 1871-1997	Images	David Downs	0 7524 1061 X	£9.99
Sheffield United FC	Images	Denis Clarebrough	0 7524 1059 8	£9.99
Sniffer (Allan Clarke)	Hb 192pp	David Saffer	0 7524 2168 9	£17.99
Southend United FC	Images	Miles & Goody	0 7524 2089 5	£9.99
The Ultimate Drop	Pb 160 pp	George Rowland (Ed.)	0 7524 2217 0	£12.99
Voices of '66	Images	Norman Shiel	0 7524 2045 3	£9.99

Introduction

There have been nearly 800 players who have played in Football and Premier League fixtures for Sheffield United and the task of selecting the 'top 100' proved to be far more difficult than I first imagined.

Andrew Kirkham, United's official statistician, kindly supplied me with a list of players in order of League appearances and, as always, I thank him for the statistics, which are mainly self-explanatory. The years quoted after the player's name and position are those when the player made his debut and his final appearance in the first team, and not when the player was first signed, or was transferred, or left the club. The column 'Other' for appearances and goals essentially refers to 'minor' competitive and war-time fixtures, and excludes friendly matches.

I decided that the first eighty from the list of appearances deserved inclusion, only to exclude three and suffer feelings of guilt. I offered friends a list of about forty other possible names, and asked them to pick their 'top twenty', and by one means and another, raised my original seventy-seven to about ninety-five and eventually to the one hundred required – but I stand ready for the brickbats which are bound to come my way, whether from former players or our supporters.

I apologise to all those omitted. Would that you all could be included, for the words 'Do you remember – ?' are rarely far away when supporters get together. I excluded some truly great players, rightly or wrongly, on the grounds that their stay was all too brief: Bruce Rioch, Ken McNaught, Paul McGrath, Dean Saunders and Gordon Cowans are just four that come to mind, and it is a fact and a problem, that in recent years, few players stay long with any club. I have also omitted all United's contemporary players other than Simon Tracey – and I'm sure his present colleagues will understand the reason for, so I believe, they all presume 'he came with the ground'.

Your choice would almost certainly have been different. Here are a few that might have been included and I wish they were: Kevin Arnott, David Barnes, Joe Bolton, Carl Bradshaw, Glenn Cockerill, Jostein Flo, Kevin Gage, John Gannon, Colin Hill, Willie Hamilton, Bob Hatton, Jim Iley, John MacPhail, Martin Pike, David Powell, Mike Trusson, Mitch Ward and Keith Waugh.

Great players from the more distant past have also been left out. A place should have been found for: Jack Almond, Len Birks, Joe Brooks, Joe Carr, Alf Common, Jack Drummond, Stan Fazackerley, Harry Hammond, George Hedley, Vince Matthews, Bobby Reid, W. Robertson, Alf Settle, Eddie Shimwell, Charlie Thompson and many others who were internationals, cup and championship winners (or just good players).

May I commend to all of you who have memories of these – and many more – former United players, a visit to the Hall of Fame at Bramall Lane, where you can see a superb collection of photographs, cups, medals, shirts, programmes and other trophies, souvenirs and ephemera. I am sure they will bring back a host of memories from the past of the ground, great games, teams and players.

The author, Denis Clarebrough.

Acknowledgements

It is now over sixty years since I was first taken to Bramall Lane, and only brief memories remain of those far-off days. My late father's reminiscences of former players and games were the background to my childhood and this book is dedicated to him.

Since those early days, it has been my privilege to meet and talk to many hundreds of players, officials, supporters and others interested in football and its past. To each and every one of them – although inevitably, some are now dead – I offer my deep gratitude. They came from all walks of life, and were not, of course, all United supporters, but they shared a love of football, the world's greatest game.

The photographs have been taken from United's growing archive, or my own collection, and I thank Sheffield Newspapers for allowing me to reproduce those for which they own the copyright.

Writing a book is somewhat of a lonely occupation and so is that of being an author's partner. My greatest thanks, therefore, go to my dear wife Maureen, who has supported and encouraged me in my work. Southampton provided the opposition on her first visit to Bramall Lane and posed a problem which was quickly spotted by her brother Ray. 'Don't you forget your roots', he reminded her, for the family come from the nearby Isle of Wight. Life being what it is, it was somehow inevitable that the Saints came out on top that day, but Maureen healed the wound by becoming a good Blade.

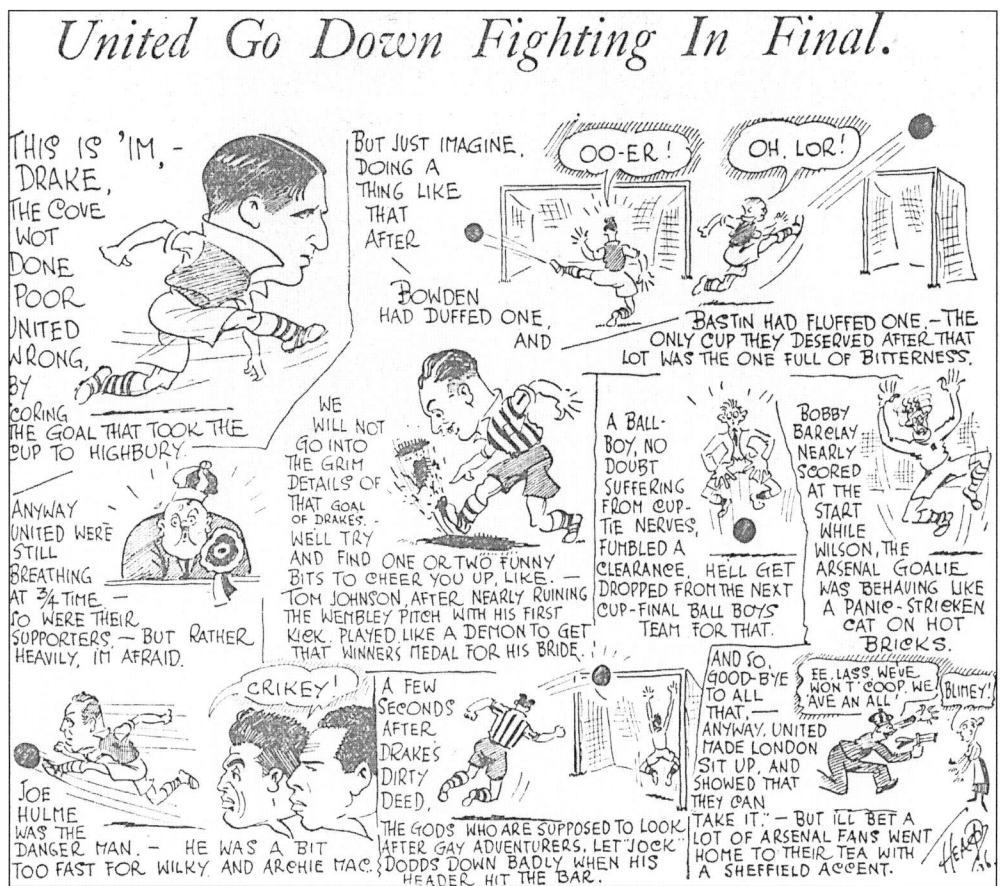

The famous Sheffied cartoonist, Harry Heap, was at the Wembley Cup Final in 1936.

100 Sheffield United Greats

Tony Agana
Len Allchurch
Len Badger
Bobby Barclay
Harold Barton
Paul Beesley
Walter Bennett
Bob Benson
Alan Birchenall
Bob Booker
Peter Boyle
Bill Brelsford
Harold Brook
Arthur Brown
Jim Brown
Ian Bryson
Ted Burgin
Bob Cain
Cec Coldwell
Colin Collindridge
Eddie Colquhoun
Bill Cook
Albert Cox
Tony Currie
Brian Deane
Bill Dearden
Jock Dodds
Jimmy Dunne
Keith Eddy
Keith Edwards
Bob Evans
John Flynn
Alex Forbes
Bill Foulke
Fred Furniss

Paul Garner
Brian Gayle
Billy Gillespie
Harold Gough
Colin Grainger
George Green
Jimmy Hagan
Derek Hawksworth
Ted Hemsley
Billy Hendry
Trevor Hockey
Glyn Hodges
Alan Hodgkinson
Bill Hodgson
David Holdsworth
Harry Hooper
Rab Howell
Tommy Hoyland
Ernest Jackson
Harry Johnson (senior)
Harry Johnson
Tom Johnson
Mick Jones
Alan Kelly
Tony Kenworthy
Keith Kettleborough
Joe Kitchen
Harry Latham
Joe Lievesley
Bert Lipsham
David Mercer
Ernest Milton
Tommy Morren
Colin Morris
Ernest Needham

Albert Nightingale
Roger Nilsen
Derek Pace
Harold Pantling
Jack Pickering
Fred Priest
Gil Reece
Brian Richardson
Walter Rickett
Alf Ringstead
Bill Russell
Geoff Salmons
Tommy Sampy
Graham Shaw
Joe Shaw
Jimmy Simmons
Ronnie Simpson
Jack Smith
Mick Speight
Paul Stancliffe
Albert Sturgess
Gerry Summers
Harry Thickett
Simon Tracey
Fred Tunstall
George Utley
Dane Whitehouse
Mick Whitham
Bernard Wilkinson
Alan Woodward

The top twenty, who appear here in italics, are covered over two pages instead of the usual one.

Tony Agana
Striker, 1988-91

	Appearances	Goals
League	118	42
FA Cup	14	5
FL Cup	12	3
Other	10	2
TOTAL	154	52

Tony Agana and Brian Deane formed an outstanding striking partnership and, in three splendid seasons under Dave Bassett, took the club from the former Third Division to the First. Sadly, Tony proved to be injury-prone and his Football League record of 60 goals in 285 appearances does scant justice to a most dangerous forward.

He was born in October 1963 in Bromley (Kent) and was on Charlton Athletic's books as a schoolboy. He played for Welling United while working for a London insurance company and had a trial with Luton Town, but a work move to Poole in Dorset led to him becoming a part-time professional with Weymouth. He had three years on the South Coast and made one appearance for the England semi-professional team. He became a full-time professional in August 1987, when he was signed by Watford's new manager Dave Bassett and, six months later, followed him to Bramall Lane.

Tony scored a late winning goal against Barnsley to mark his debut, but the season ended with relegation. It had been a sad first season for Agana as a full-time pro. He had generally played down the flanks, but Bassett thought he might be more successful playing in a more central striking role. An opportunity came in the first match of the new season, when Tony came on as substitute to play alongside Deane and the pair immediately looked at home.

Tony had tremendous pace and could twist and turn at a speed, which was an asset that defenders found difficult to deal with. Deane and Agana could both hold the ball and bring others into play and both were good finishers – many of Deane's goals came from Agana's flick-ons. They scored nearly 60 League and Cup goals that season, including a dual hat-trick against Chester. Tony's 24 League goals included another hat-trick in the last home match and a goal at Molineux to clinch a return to the Second Division. Of particular merit was a superb goal against Huddersfield in the FA Cup. Twelve months later, United returned to the top flight of English football when Agana scored two goals in a vital and dramatic 5-2 victory at Leicester in the final match of the season.

Tony should have been at his peak at this time, but injuries began to be a serious problem and he missed a growing number of games. Furthermore, when he did play, the sparkle seemed to have gone. United, therefore, might have considered themselves fortunate when he was transferred to Notts County in November 1991 for a fee in the range of £680,000 to £750,000. The move was less than successful as Notts were twice relegated. He had a loan spell at Leeds and later played for Hereford United, Cliftonville, Leek Town and Guisley.

Len Allchurch
Outside right, 1961-65

	Appearances	Goals
League	123	32
FA Cup	12	2
FL Cup	9	2
Other	2	1
TOTAL	146	37

Few new players can have had such a dramatic immediate influence on a club's fortunes as that made by Welsh international right winger, Len Allchurch, when he joined United in March 1961 for a fee of £12,500. United had reached the semi-final of the FA Cup but their promotion challenge was faltering as the team struggled to score goals. A vital match had been lost against Ipswich, the eventual champions, and the lack of a satisfactory outside right had become an all-too-obvious weakness.

Len had been born in Swansea in September 1933 and was a younger brother of Ivor, the Swans' international inside forward. He joined his brother at the Vetch Field and had made 272 League appearances in the old Second Division when he came to the Lane. In all those years, Swansea had never made a serious promotion challenge and so the incentive for Len to join his brother in the First Division by helping United win promotion was obvious. The little winger was an inspiration, scoring on his debut in a 2-1 victory at Leeds and adding four more goals in the next five games to take United back to the top flight. In a strange quirk of fate, Newcastle United, where Ivor Allchurch was a star, were relegated, though Len and Ivor did play against each other in the following season in the Football League Cup.

Len had won 7 caps with Swansea and added 4 more with United. He was a delightful player to watch: quick-thinking, two-footed and very clever. He had a very deceptive body swerve and close ball control and, when he cut in towards the goal, Len made splendid openings for his colleagues and could finish with firm authority. He may have been small, but he could also resist a challenge and he was calm and collected – it was claimed that in twenty years of League football, he was never cautioned or booked.

He was transferred to Stockport County in September 1965 and was a member of their Fourth Division championship team and then returned to Swansea, winning promotion in 1970 with his old team before joining Haverford West and playing once more with Ivor.

Len Badger
Right-back, 1962-75

	Appearances	Goals
League	458	7
FA Cup	24	0
FL Cup	30	0
Other	29	1
TOTAL	541	8

Len Badger, who was born in Sheffield in June 1945, became one of United's most stylish full-backs. He fully deserved the representative honours that came his way but, perhaps because he was rather small in stature and was judged to lack a little in confidence – which was not obvious to spectators – he missed out on full England honours.

Len had played at right half or inside right for his school, but was used at right-back by Sheffield, Yorkshire and England boys and went on to play for the England youth team – with fellow United full-back Bernard Shaw – when they won the European tournament at Wembley in 1963. Although he was less than average height, Len played with calm authority, invariably attempted to use the ball well and was always quick in recovery. He graduated to the England under-23 team when he was still essentially a United reserve player and made 13 appearances at that level.

Badger and Bernard Shaw made their first-team debuts at the Lane when they were still seventeen, towards the end of April 1963 in a First Division match against Leyton Orient. Len was a mature footballer for his age and a good listener – he would acknowledge his debt to Cec Coldwell, his predecessor at right-back in the United team, and to Joe Shaw, who both watched over the advancement of all the fine young players that United had in those days. Shaw's belief was 'Get it down, control it, stroke it around' and that was Len's way of playing, although John Harris, the United manager, might also be saying, 'Don't take chances. Get it up-field as far as you can.'

Len became United's regular right-back towards the end of the 1963/64 season, and was soon spoken of as a future England defender. He was near to a place in the full England team but, when George Cohen, the regular England right-back, was injured in 1967, it was Cyril Knowles and Keith Newton who were chosen, Len having to be satisfied with further appearances in the under-23 team and 3 appearances for the Football League.

Len was a fine full-back and a pleasure to watch. He had been given the position of United captain by John Harris in January 1966 and he captained the side for the first time in a First Division match at the City Ground in Nottingham. At first sight, it seemed an extraordinary choice – for Badger was still only twenty and had never acted as captain at any junior level – but the young player had no hesitation in accepting the position and looked forward to the challenge.

The Blades were relegated in 1968, how-

Len takes a shot at goal against Sunderland in February 1971. Trevor Hockey looks on.

ever, and, not long into the new season, Arthur Rowley, the new team manager, gave the captain's role to Eddie Colquhoun, whom he had just signed from West Brom. United supporters could still delight in Badger's polished displays and will particularly remember Len in the 'You can do magic' team of the early 1970s, which had returned to the old First Division and played with such a flowing and entertaining style.

Len was always prepared to attack and would have taken to the modern idea of a wing-back like a duck to water. He had played in more advanced positions as a schoolboy and, partly for that reason, Len had fourteen games in the number eight shirt in the autumn of 1972, with Steve Goulding playing at right-back, but the experiment couldn't be called a success.

United made a disastrous start to the 1975/76 season and Ken Furphy, the manager (who would soon be sacked), felt that Badger, because of his age, physique and declining stamina, could no longer hold down a permanent first-team position. Len missed a few games and, soon after the arrival of the new manager, Jimmy Sirrel, Badger was transferred to Chesterfield. Joe Shaw, United's former centre half, was now the manager of the Derbyshire club and he signed Len in January 1976 at a fee of £3,000 and made him the captain, although his playing days came to an end in 1978 after two serious injuries. These days, Len keeps the Fox & Goose, a handsome inn on the edge of Old Brampton, about four miles to the west of Chesterfield.

Bobby Barclay
Inside forward, 1931-37 and 1944-45

	Appearances	Goals
League	231	67
FA Cup	18	3
FL Cup	-	-
Other	15	7
TOTAL	264	77

Bobby Barclay and Jack Pickering, United's inside forwards in the 1936 FA Cup final, were both English internationals. United were defeated by the Arsenal and, two years later, Barclay, who by then had been transferred to Huddersfield Town, suffered the same sad fate once more, when his new club lost in the final to a last-minute Preston North End penalty kick.

Born in Scotswood, Newcastle-on-Tyne, in October 1906, Barclay joined Derby County in 1927 and came to Bramall Lane in 1931 when he was twenty-four, for the then considerable fee of £3,500. A clever and unselfish inside forward and also a good marksman (Barclay had scored 23 goals in 61 League appearances for Derby), he soon settled into the United team and provided many of the openings that led to goals for Jimmy Dunne and later for Jock Dodds.

First capped by England in 1931 against Northern Ireland, Barclay won two further caps against Scotland in 1932 and 1936 and appeared in the 1936 FA Cup final for United against Arsenal. United had narrowly failed to secure a return to the former First Division in 1936, and a poor away record ended their hopes in the following season. Davison, the manager, decided to make changes and, to the dismay of most of United's supporters, Barclay and Eddie Boot, a promising young half-back, were sold to Huddersfield Town for £7,000 and both appeared in the 1938 Cup Final against Preston North End.

Barclay's last appearance for the Huddersfield first team was in April 1944, but he returned to the Lane during the 1944/45 season, making 8 guest appearances for United and scoring 5 goals, and it was fitting that the last of those should be at the Baseball Ground, where his career as a professional player had begun. He was transferred by the Leeds Road club in 1946 to Hurst, a Cheshire League side, but returned to Huddersfield to join the training staff. He died there in July 1969.

Harold Barton
Outside right, 1934-43

	Appearances	Goals
League	184	41
FA Cup	19	5
FL Cup	-	-
Other	87	28
TOTAL	290	74

Harold Barton, United's outside right in the 1936 FA Cup final, had pace, skill and a powerful shot. He could thrill the crowds and might have been one of the finest right wingers in the game, but he lacked that final ounce of grit, determination and devil that would have made him into a truly great player.

He was born in Leigh in Lancashire on the last day of September in 1911, but his boyhood was spent in Blackpool. He became a professional player with Liverpool in 1928 and began to hold down a regular first-team spot late in 1930. His place in the history of the Anfield club is secure, for he scored a hat-trick against Everton in 1933 and he also netted four at Saltergate in an FA Cup tie.

Harold lost his first-team place in the Liverpool team and was transferred to United in the close season of 1934 for £1,600. Barton was twenty-three when he came to the Lane and United were starting their first Second Division campaign since 1893. For the next five years, Harold was United's regular outside right and he gave some brilliant displays. He had a tremendous burst of speed, a fluid body swerve and fine ball control and his centres and shooting were hard and accurate. During the FA Cup final in 1936, it was from his fine run and centre that Dodds hit the face of the Arsenal cross-bar and so nearly equalised; Harold was also a member of the 1939 promotion team.

There was, however, another side to Barton during his time at the Lane. He asked for a transfer in 1935 and another request for a transfer in January 1939 followed derisory remarks from the crowd, who were well aware, as were his colleagues, of the player's strengths and weaknesses.

Barton had lost his place to Alf Jeffries when the start of the war curtailed the 1939/40 season, and he missed all of the 1940/41 United fixtures. He played regularly during the next two seasons, however, and had a fine record from the penalty spot. His last appearance in United colours was in 1943 but he continued to play as a guest player, assisting Bradford Park Avenue, Lincoln City, Chesterfield, Wednesday and Rotherham United (he once scored a hat trick of penalties for the Millmoor side). He was officially released by United in 1945 and, for a short spell, played for Denaby United. In later years, Barton kept a pub in Sheffield and was a keen onlooker at the Lane for many years.

Paul Beesley
Defender, 1990-95

	Appearances	Goals
League	168	7
FA Cup	11	1
FL Cup	13	0
Other	3	1
TOTAL	195	9

Signed in July 1990 by Dave Bassett, the United manager, to strengthen his squad of players after securing promotion to the old First Division, Paul Beesley proved to be a determined defender and his consistent performances finally silenced those critics who felt that he would not be successful at the highest echelon of League football.

Paul was born in July 1965 and grew up in the Walton district of Liverpool. By the time he was eighteen, he was playing as a part-timer for the nearby Marine club. He became a Wigan Athletic player in the summer of 1984, but it was not until April 1986 that he secured a permanent first-team place. He made over 170 appearances for the Lancashire club before his transfer in October 1989 to Leyton Orient for a club record fee of £175,000.

Only nine months after that move to Brisbane Road, Beesley headed north for Bramall Lane for a fee in the region of £350,000 to £375,000. He could play in any defensive position on the left side, whether in a central partnership, or at left-back, or in the middle of the park. In his first year, playing in the old First Division, he settled into playing as a central defender, taking the place of Paul Stancliffe and then Mark Morris and, in his second season, he enjoyed a successful partnership with Brian Gayle at the heart of the defence.

A turning point in his time at the Lane came when United met Blackburn Rovers in the sixth round of the FA Cup in March 1993. Paul found himself on the substitutes' bench and he failed to make the squad for the semi-final clash with Wednesday. Beesley was brought back into the team, frequently playing at left-back, but an automatic first-team spot had gone.

Paul gave United excellent service, although he was never an elegant player and was very dependent on his left foot. He lacked a bit of pace, but played sensibly within his limitations. He read the game well, tackled keenly and effectively; his heading was good and he was strong, dependable and consistent.

Beesley joined Leeds United in August 1995 for a fee of £250,000 and moved to Manchester City in 1997 for £500,000. He had loan spells with Port Vale – later moving there on a free transfer – and West Bromwich Albion and also played for Blackpool and Chester.

Walter Bennett
Outside right, 1896-1905

	Appearances	Goals
League	195	59
FA Cup	37	11
FL Cup	-	-
Other	2	0
TOTAL	234	70

Only Alan Woodward, who was a very similar player, could have some claim to challenge Walter Bennett for the title of United's greatest outside right. Both were thrilling players to watch when they were in the right mood.

Bennett was born in April 1874 in Mexborough, and joined United in January 1896 from the local club (who were an important team in those days in South Yorkshire). He had scored 87 of the 123 Mexborough goals in the previous season but had rejected an offer from Derby County, deciding on his father's advice to complete an apprenticeship. A columnist in a Sheffield newspaper was not impressed with the news that he had joined United. 'From what I know of Bennett, £10 seems a long price to pay.' The fee may have been £40, but the comment seemed reasonable at the time, as Bennett at first was slow and his health was poor, but by 1897 he had shed two stone in weight and was proving to be an outstanding winger.

He played a major part in the capture of the League Championship in 1898 and the FA Cup in the following year. He was capped twice by England in 1901, when United were FA Cup finalists, but missed the replay of the 1902 Cup Final victory, having been injured in the first game (although United secured permission from the FA to present him with a winners' medal). He was transfer listed in 1903, but persuaded United to re-engage him and was eventually transferred to Bristol City in April 1905 for £50 and was a member of their Second Division championship side.

Although he had always been known as 'Cocky', Walter was a man of moods and wasn't consistent. He was, however, often an extremely dangerous opponent and 'irresistible on his day'. His build was stocky and thick set, but he was fast, a good dribbler and could put across accurate centres at a height and speed that defenders hated, but which were meat and drink to the United forwards of the time. Bennett was also an excellent finisher, whether closing in with the ball at his feet or in meeting centres from the opposite wing, and had one of the hardest shots in the game.

On leaving Bristol he returned to South Yorkshire, playing again for Mexborough and Denaby. Sadly, he was killed in a roof collapse at Denaby Main colliery on 6 April 1908.

Bob Benson
Full-back, 1905-13

	Appearances	Goals
League	273	20
FA Cup	10	1
FL Cup	-	-
Other	2	0
TOTAL	285	21

Bob Benson will always be remembered for his penalty kicks and because of his death in the dressing room at Highbury after a game played during the First World War.

Benson was born in the Cumbrian port of Whitehaven, but his family moved to the Dunston and Swalwell area, near Gateshead. He came to the attention of Newcastle United and spent two seasons with the Tyneside club, making a single League appearance, before being transferred to Southampton in September 1904.

United sought his transfer in May 1905 and were fortunate in that the Saints asked for a modest fee, for they were under the impression that United would also have to pay a Football League transfer fee to Newcastle, but the Tyneside club had allowed his League registration to lapse.

A two-footed player, Benson first played for United at left-back but switched to the right in his first season, only returning to the left in 1912. He took over the captaincy in 1913, but a rare injury cost him his place in the team and the form of Jack English, who took his place, was so good that he asked for a transfer. He was keen to return to the south of England and was sold to the Arsenal in November 1913 for £600.

Sturdily built with light hair, Bob was a fine footballer, but he was a player of moods and always nervous before a game. Contemporary reports describe him as 'dashing and brilliant' and a 'tower of strength'. His tackling and kicking were excellent and he was 'a fine header of the ball' but he could be 'impetuous' and 'inclined to wander' and, after completing a tour of South Africa with the FA in 1910, further honours were limited to a single cap against Ireland in 1913. He had a fine record with penalty kicks and will always be remembered because he began his run at the ball from near the halfway line, relying on a colleague to place the ball on the spot.

Transferred to the Arsenal, Bob's last Football League appearance came in April 1915. Playing at centre forward, he scored twice, never having previously played in a forward position. He didn't play again until 19 February 1916. He hadn't trained for many months, but Arsenal were short of players and Bob volunteered to turn out. The exertion proved too much and, with about half an hour left to play, he was forced to leave the field. He walked off the pitch but died in the dressing room shortly after the game had finished. He was buried in his Arsenal shirt.

Alan Birchenall
Striker, 1964-67

	Appearances	Goals
League	107	31
FA Cup	8	2
FL Cup	6	2
Other	3	2
TOTAL	124	37

Alan Birchenall was just one of that extraordinary group of young players who came together at Bramall Lane in the early and mid-1960s and formed the bulk of the United First Division side. He was an immediate success and his transfer to Chelsea in November 1967, soon after that of Mick Jones to Leeds United, was a bitter blow.

Alan was born in the East End of London in August 1945 but his family moved to Nottingham when he was still only four years of age. He played for Nottingham boys and also for the County Schools, but he almost ended any possible career as a professional player by rejecting overtures from Nottingham Forest and gave up playing for the Notts County Midland Intermediate side because County couldn't afford to employ him on their ground staff.

He came to United's attention while playing for Thorneywood Athletic and was a prolific scorer for United in the 1963/64 season in the Northern Intermediate League team. He made his first-team debut at Stoke in September 1964 and, three days later, scored both United goals in the 2-0 victory against the Owls at Hillsborough and had ten goals to his credit after playing in thirteen games. Birchenall certainly enjoyed playing against the Wednesday, netting six goals on his first four outings against them. He didn't maintain that rate of scoring, but Jones and Birchenall, when playing up front together, were a dangerous striking partnership.

He was awarded two England under-23 international caps when he was with United and two more with Chelsea, but further honours eluded him. Alan was an outgoing personality in an age when Alf Ramsay was the England manager and it perhaps hindered his football career. His scoring rate also fell away at Stamford Bridge. Birchenall had never considered himself a 'natural goal-scorer' – which seems strange considering the huge number he scored as a youngster, but one can't argue with the fact that, in general, the more coaching he received, the fewer goals he scored.

He was transferred to Crystal Palace in 1970 and a year later to Leicester City, the fees in both instances being of the order of £100,000. He played in a more withdrawn position in his six seasons at Filbert Street and, after a loan spell with Notts County, he played in the United States for San Jose and Memphis.

He had brief stints with Blackburn, Luton, Hereford and Trowbridge, before returning to Leicester City in a commercial role involving public relations.

Bob Booker
Midfielder, 1988-91

	Appearances	Goals
League	109	13
FA Cup	10	0
FL Cup	4	0
Other	8	1
TOTAL	131	14

There was little (or perhaps nothing) in the playing career of Bob Booker before he joined United from Brentford which would have indicated that his three seasons at Bramall Lane would be filled with such drama and would make him a hero to so many United supporters.

Booker was born in Watford in January 1958 and became an apprentice in the upholstery trade. He joined Brentford in October 1978 as a striker and was loaned for a short time to Barnet. He was tall, willing and strong and would play in most positions on the field, though increasingly appearing in midfield. He gave fine service to Brentford for eleven seasons, making nearly 250 League appearances and scoring 42 goals. His career however, had appeared to be winding down, following a ligament injury in 1986.

Fate plays funny tricks. In November 1988, United's Simon Webster broke his leg in a cup-tie at Mansfield and Dave Bassett, moved quickly to bring Booker – his Brentford contract allowed him a free transfer if he chose to leave – to the Lane. Brentford, in Booker's time, had been a Third Division team but had achieved little. United, on the other hand were second in the table and had more potential. Booker was thirty and had been contemplating a transfer to Barnet and a contract cleaning business, but Bassett was offering him a new lease of life. He seized his opportunity, though it took a time to conquer his critics for he was rusty and 'had never pretended to be one of the most skilful players'.

Those critics grew fewer in number, and his enthusiastic, wholehearted displays played a massive part in two promotion campaigns that took the Blades back to the top flight of English football and he had the honour, in Stancliffe's absence because of injury, of captaining the side in the final three games – including that joyous day at Leicester when promotion was achieved with a remarkable 5-2 victory.

Bob made 41 appearances in the former First Division before returning, in November 1991, to Brentford. What he had achieved was quite remarkable and he forged a bond with United's supporters that was expressed so clearly when his departure from the Lane was announced. He was a good all round footballer and a model professional but, when his career seemed all but over, he achieved so much more because of his enthusiasm, dedication and commitment to United's cause.

A knee injury brought his playing career to an end – other than a few games with Harrow Borough – but he returned to Brentford as a coach before becoming the assistant manager at Brighton.

Peter Boyle
Full-back, 1898-1904

	Appearances	Goals
League	150	1
FA Cup	34	0
FL Cup	-	-
Other	3	0
TOTAL	187	1

Peter Boyle and Harry Johnson (senior) both played in the United FA Cup victories of 1899 and 1902 and lived to see a son win an FA Cup medal in 1925. Peter Boyle was the club's first Irish international and a tough full-back who gave his opponents and, at the end of his days at the Lane, the United committee, plenty of headaches.

Boyle was born in Carlingford in County Louth, but his family moved to Scotland when he was a child. He played for Albion Rovers and was transferred to Sunderland in December 1896. His staunch displays for Sunderland in 1898 against United, when they won the League Championship, didn't go unnoticed and he was signed at the end of that year for £175. He took the left-back position from Pilgrim and Simpson, who had proved inadequate deputies for Bob Cain.

Boyle was an immediate success at the Lane, winning an FA Cup medal at the end of that season and added a second in 1902 to the runners-up medal of the previous year. He was awarded 5 Irish caps but was selected on several other occasions, rejecting the opportunity in order to play for United, the club making financial restitution (as was common in those days).

He was often described as a 'robust' type of player, but 'dirty' has also appeared in print. Contemporaries commented on his 'devil may care' attitude and all agreed that his kicking was top class and that he was a fine tackler and a determined opponent.

Relations between the club and the player deteriorated during the 1903/04 season and he was twice suspended for misconduct. He claimed that he had been promised a benefit, which United denied, and the club issued a statement declaring that 'more consideration and lenient treatment had been shown to Boyle than any other player.'

He joined Motherwell in May 1904 for £100 but returned to England one year later, joining Clapton Orient when they secured entry to the Second Division. He later played for Wigan Town, Chorley, Eccles Borough and Abertillery, and had a few months in 1912 as the player-manager of York City. For much of this time, he worked as a miner and he later played for and coached the Brodsworth Colliery team. He died in Doncaster in 1939 and his age was given as sixty-two at the time.

Bill Brelsford
Defender, 1909-22

	Appearances	Goals
League	277	1
FA Cup	19	0
FL Cup	-	-
Other	121	1
TOTAL	417	2

All successful football teams need a 'strong man' in midfield and Bill Brelsford supplied that inestimable quality for United over many seasons. Brought up in the Darnall district of Sheffield, he first came to prominence with Doncaster Rovers, who were then playing in the Midland League, before signing for United in the close season of 1909.

Although he had previously played as a centre half – in those days a more attacking role – Brelsford made his debut for United at right half in the opening match of the season at Middlesbrough and was an immediate success. He remained a regular first-team player, playing at right half or centre half, until 1921.

Bill wasn't tall but he was a fine header of the ball, timing his jumps to be a fraction after his opponent but, above all, he was a totally committed player with stamina and great strength in his shoulders, which he used to good effect. He covered well and he wasn't an easy man to pass; the only weakness in his game lay in his passing, which was no more than adequate.

He was a very physical player but honest. Inevitably, however, matters occasionally got out of hand when Brelsford played. He had some tremendous battles with Teddy Glennon, a Wednesday player of similar style, and the pair of them were sent off during the infamous derby game of January 1916. Bill's nose was broken in a similar game at Leeds when, in Brelsford's words, 'I don't know what caused the bother. Something went wrong and bang went the apple cart.'

In fact, there were more than an few apple carts turned over during Bill's playing career, but he always played a vital part in the United defence of those days and never more so than in the successful 1915 FA Cup campaign. Soon after his playing days were over, he joined the United training staff and remained at the Lane until the outbreak of war in 1939, when he became master of the kennels at the Darnall greyhound track. He died in Sheffield in March 1954.

Harold Brook
Inside forward, 1940-54

	Appearances	Goals
League	229	89
FA Cup	20	9
FL Cup	-	-
Other	40	13
TOTAL	289	111

Harold Brook was born in Sheffield in October 1921 and played for Sheffield Boys at both cricket and football. He played football for Woodbourn Alliance between the ages of sixteen and eighteen, and signed amateur forms for United. Brook was soon playing for United at both cricket and football, but no player can have made such contrasting debuts, scoring a fine century for a United team at cricket but tasting defeat at football. The match was against Lincoln City in September 1940, with Brook at left-back, and United lost 9-2!

Harold next played for Fulwood, which was run in those early war years as a United nursery team, before joining the RAF in 1941. He was stationed at Weeton in Lancashire and it was there that he developed into an inside forward and made occasional appearances for Manchester United.

Brook began to play regularly for United in the latter part of the 1945/46 season, when the club won the League North championship. He played several games for the Blades at wing half, but will mainly be remembered as an inside forward. He was fast, direct and had a fierce shot and he combined with Jimmy Hagan to form a perfect inside forward duo. With two speedy and dangerous wingers in Ringstead and Hawksworth and the line well led by Len Browning, the five forwards formed an exciting attack.

Brook was then at his best. 'The trouble with football,' he once told me, 'is that by the time you know how to play, you're too old' – indeed 'Brooky' was a more confident and much better player when he was twenty-eight than he had been as a younger man.

United were foolish to 'sell' Brook to Leeds United in 1954 – the £600 fee would be Brook's accrued share of benefit – but United acted on medical advice that turned out to be wrong. Leeds United thought Brook might last six months but, in the event, he had more than three seasons at Elland Road with barely a hint of knee trouble and his partnership with John Charles brought the bulk of the goals that took Leeds United back to the First Division in 1956. Leeds then recouped their £600 outlay when they transferred Brook in 1958 to Lincoln City. Harold later ran a successful business in Sheffield and died in his native city in November 1998.

Arthur Brown
Centre forward, 1902-08

	Appearances	Goals
League	178	100
FA Cup	9	4
FL Cup	-	-
Other	-	-
TOTAL	187	104

One of the youngest ever players to play for England, Arthur Brown was a fine centre forward who joined United at a time when the great team which had come together at the end of the nineteenth century had passed its peak, and his career at the Lane ended when he was transferred to Sunderland after an acrimonious dispute.

He was born in Gainsborough in April 1885 and educated at the local grammar school. Brown joined Gainsborough Trinity, who were then in the old Second Division, and made his debut on the day before his seventeenth birthday. He was transferred to United in May 1902, after playing just three Football League games for the Trinity, in which he had scored two goals.

He was remarkably mature for his age, and very fast, and had the ability to stop dead in his tracks. Brown led the forward line with skill and judgment but, above all, 'he was an opportunist' with 'a wonderful shot'. On his day, there was no finer centre forward, but he 'often failed to give of his best'. He was still only eighteen when he was awarded the first of his two international caps and he had a benefit (£232) when he was twenty-three years old.

His transfer to Sunderland in June 1908 caused enormous bitterness and ill-feeling. Brown had informed United that he wanted to devote time to the family business in Gainsborough and requested a transfer to the Lincolnshire club; failing that, he would retire from the game. Eventually, he re-signed for United but insisted on going on the open-to-transfer list. United accepted a League record fee of £1,600 from Sunderland and the matter of the family business was never mentioned. At an FA enquiry, Trinity were found not guilty of 'poaching', but Brown's evidence was regarded as 'unsatisfactory' and he had to pay the costs of the FA Commission.

A little more than two years later, Brown was transferred to Fulham. In April 1912, he moved to Middlesbrough and then, after just four games, he retired. Brown was only twenty-seven when his first-class playing days came to an end. He returned to Gainsborough and, in 1919, acted as an 'adviser' to the Trinity. His brother, Fred, also played for United, first as a guest player in 1915 and then between 1919 and 1923. Arthur died in the place of his birth in 1944.

Jim Brown
Goalkeeper, 1974-78

	Appearances	Goals
League	170	0
FA Cup	6	0
FL Cup	7	0
Other	20	0
TOTAL	203	0

United's Scottish international goalkeeper made a curious entry into the Football League, for he made his League debut twice. Jim was born in Coatbridge in May 1952 and joined the local Scottish League side, Albion Rovers. He was transferred to Chesterfield in December 1972 and made his debut at Blackburn on Boxing Day, Chesterfield winning 2-1 and played again, four days later, at Saltergate. It was then discovered that his registration papers had been held up in the Christmas post and the Blackburn match had to be replayed (to their credit, Chesterfield won again).

Ken Furphy, the United manager, who had been in charge at Blackburn, didn't forget Brown, and in March 1974 brought him to the Lane. He made his debut with Tony Field at Maine Road. United ultimately paid about £80,000 for Jim, who proved to be an excellent shot stopper and was capped by Scotland against Romania in 1975.

Brown was never content when fellow Scot, Jimmy Sirrel, was the United manager but the turning point in Jim's stay at the Lane came at the beginning of the 1978/79 season, when he lost his first-team place to Steve Conroy. He became one of the many players who moved to the United States, playing with Eddie Colquhoun for Detroit Express and then Washington Diplomats, before a final move to Chicago Sting. He returned to Britain in 1982 and trained in Chesterfield, signing non-contract forms with Kettering and a month-by-month contract with Cardiff City.

Ian Porterfield brought Jim back to the Lane on deadline day in March 1983 as injury cover and he played once in the Central League. He became a Chesterfield player again in July of that year, scoring a goal with a drop-kick against Stockport County – he had scored his first in the USA – and, three years later, was appointed commercial manager (although he was retained as a player and played regularly for the first team until December 1988).

Jim retained his position on the commercial side at Saltergate when he finished as a professional player, but continued to enjoy the game, playing centre forward for a Sunday League team. He said he preferred that position, 'So that I can get my own back!'

Ian Bryson
Outside left/utility forward, 1988-93

	Appearances	Goals
League	155	36
FA Cup	22	4
FL Cup	13	1
Other	10	3
TOTAL	200	44

Ian was one of Dave Bassett's 'new' team that was forged in 1988 after relegation to the Third Division. He was a typical Bassett signing – offering skill but, above all, commitment, loyalty and the willingness to battle on when the cause seemed lost.

He was born in Kilmarnock in November 1962 and became a part-time player with 'Killie' in 1981, making 250 League and cup appearances and scoring 44 goals. Working on a farm kept him fit, but he wanted to try his luck as a full-timer in England. He was beginning to feel that, at twenty-five years of age, he wasn't going to realize his football aspirations. In August 1988, however, United took him on trial in Sweden and signed him as a full-time professional, paying a fee of £40,000.

It was an opportunity that Bryson grasped with both hands. He played at outside left in the first match of the season and was a regular first-team player for four campaigns. He usually attacked down the left side but would give of his best in any forward position and, later, often appeared in the centre forward position.

His excellent work helped take United into the old First Division and he scored vital goals, including last-minute penalty kicks at Brighton and Barnsley. It was Ian who gave United a last opportunity of retaining their hard-earned First Division place in 1990. Four points from the first sixteen games had been a disastrous start, but his two goals against Forest – he also saw a volley hit both posts and come out – helped the Blades to victory and his four goals in March were all critical, bringing in twelve points and eventual survival.

Ian was a strong, hardworking player who always gave one hundred per cent. He was good in the air, had a powerful shot and crossed well and he was dangerous cutting in and in meeting centres from the other wing. He was also a man who showed what guts and determination could do when players with greater ball skills failed. Bassett described him as 'honest, willing and conscientious' and it is noteworthy that of all the players who began the League season in 1988, Bryson was the last to leave Bramall Lane.

He was transferred to Barnsley in August 1993 for £20,000, but three months later joined Preston North End (£42,500) and captained the club when they won the Third Division championship, before moving to Rochdale in 1997.

Ted Burgin
Goalkeeper, 1949-57

	Appearances	Goals
League	281	0
FA Cup	20	0
FL Cup	-	-
Other	13	0
TOTAL	314	0

Ted Burgin was undoubtedly one of United's finest goalkeepers and well deserved the nickname of 'The Cat' which some of his playing contemporaries bestowed upon him. His playing career at the Lane was not, however, one of unmitigated joy and success and this led to transfer requests and a feeling that he had suffered more than his fair share of ill-luck.

Born in April 1927, Ted became a professional player in unusual circumstances. Playing for the Lincolnshire side, Alford Town, he found the travelling from his home near Sheffield difficult and wrote to Teddy Davison, the United manager, asking for a trial – without mentioning that he was a 5ft 7in goalkeeper. Burgin had written to the right man, for Davison, of similar height, was a former England custodian and signed Burgin at the end of the month's trial.

Burgin's agility and athleticism was immediately obvious and, after only three games of the new season, he was given his first-team debut at Swansea and immediately made the position his own. He established a position as United's fittest player. 'A fitness fanatic' was the description of one contemporary and he was usually first home in training runs around the Bramall Lane cricket field or in short sprints. His pace in coming out of goal proved disconcerting to many forwards and his punching and catching were excellent.

His ability didn't go unnoticed: he went on two FA tours, won England 'B' caps and, for a time, was the England reserve goalkeeper, but there were flaws in his makeup and technique. He was unlucky with injuries, suffering upwards of twenty fractures during his career, had frequent brushes with authority (he could be outspoken) and he made several transfer requests, although his playing colleagues never had anything but praise for his skill as a 'keeper.

Burgin was an ever-present during the Second Division championship season of 1952/53, but lost his first-team place to Alan Hodgkinson and was sold to Doncaster Rovers in December 1957 for £3,000. After only five appearances, he broke his collar bone and was transferred to Leeds United. In Ted's second season at Elland Road, Leeds United were relegated and Burgin moved to Rochdale, where he eventually made 234 League and Cup appearances.

Bob Cain
Full-back, 1891-98

	Appearances	Goals
League	164	3
FA Cup	14	0
FL Cup	-	-
Other	42	0
TOTAL	220	3

Bob Cain was the only ever-present in United's successful Championship campaign of 1897/98, and yet he chose that moment to leave Bramall Lane, a move that he came to bitterly regret.

Cain was born in Slamannan in 1866 and, after playing for his local side, joined nearby Airdrie. Then (still as an amateur) he went on the books of Glasgow Rangers, before heading south into England in 1889 to become a professional. Bob had one season in the Football League with Everton and then joined Bootle, the other major Merseyside club of that time. In the summer of 1891, Bob joined United and played that season at right-back. When entry was secured to the Football League in 1892, he switched to the left-back position.

There can be no doubts that he was a fine player and he missed very few games. In 1916, a respected journalist wrote that Cain had been the 'best Sheffield left-back' and, three years later, another wrote that Cain was '... a bit of human oak. His game was strength personified. He kicked brilliantly without a semblance of effort. He tackled shrewdly and generally fairly' – although this writer admitted that he wasn't 'sure if Cain or Boyle had been the best back in Sheffield'.

The 1897/98 First Division triumph marked the peak of Cain's playing career. He had played in the Scottish international trial in March but was tempted at the beginning of May 1898 by an approach from Tottenham Hotspur, who were members of the Southern League and could sign Football League players without having to pay a transfer fee. How much Cain received is disputed, but he joined the London club and lived to regret it.

Cain was not happy in London and wrote to United seeking to return, but was turned down. United cancelled an order for his championship medal and withdrew a £20 benefit bonus. It was generally felt that he had treated United shabbily and the £250 transfer fee that United were reported to be seeking from Football League clubs was regarded as reasonable. Cain, no doubt feeling very low, returned to Scotland and played for Albion Rovers but in November, United, hoping to receive some return for their player, accepted a £75 transfer fee from Small Heath – although Cain made no FA Cup or League appearances for the Birmingham club.

Cec Coldwell
Right-back, 1952-66

	Appearances	Goals
League	410	2
FA Cup	41	0
FL Cup	10	0
Other	18	0
TOTAL	479	2

Cec Coldwell was one of United's longest-serving and most respected captains. In his early years, few could have forecast that Cec Coldwell would have a long and fine career in football. His talents were comparatively modest, but he had the right attitude, a willingness to listen to advice and to know that there is always more to learn about the game. He trained hard and worked with a real determination and succeeded where hundreds of others failed.

He was born in Dungworth in January 1929 and played for a local work's team. Cec attended a few evening training sessions at Bramall Lane but his talents didn't shine brightly enough to attract attention. A trial with Bradford City was more successful but he 'didn't like the look of the place so went back home.'

Cec then joined the Norton Woodseats Club, was spotted by Sheffield United and, in September 1951, at the age of twenty-one, became a United professional and played in the Central League side. His play slowly improved and he made his first-team debut in his customary right-back position in April 1952, but he didn't feature again in the League side until October 1953 and it was not until 1955 that he finally replaced Fred Furniss as United's regular right-back.

Coldwell learned a lot from Furniss, from Reg Freeman, the United manager who succeeded Davison, and from Joe Mercer, the former England captain, who became manager in the summer of 1955. It was Mercer who appointed Coldwell as team captain and created and coached the famous United defence that served the club so well in the League and regular FA Cup campaigns. Joe was a shrewd judge of character: he liked the new captain's 'attitude to the game' and Coldwell, throughout his thirty-two years at the Lane as a player, coach and acting manager, never wavered in having the right approach.

He led the team to promotion and the FA Cup semi-final in 1961, before retiring as a player in 1966. He joined the coaching staff and took charge of the first team in 1969 and had two spells as caretaker-manager before standing down in 1983.

Those who speak of soccer as a simple game would have no hesitation in choosing Cec as one of their favourite players. He read the game well, anticipated the opposition's moves and rarely was beaten either by trickery or speed. He tackled with strength and covered well and used the ball simply and effectively. Cec wasn't stylish in the way one admired in the play of Joe and Graham Shaw, but he was totally sound and reliable.

Colin Collindridge
Left-winger/centre forward, 1939-50

	Appearances	Goals
League	142	52
FA Cup	10	6
FL Cup	-	-
Other	80	37
TOTAL	232	95

The outbreak of war in 1939 could not have occurred at a worse time for Collindridge, for he was eighteen years old and beginning to make his mark in the reserve team. The war, however, did provide opportunities for young players and three weeks after the declaration, Collindridge was given a first-team debut at Huddersfield, held his place and, at the end of that season, had scored an impressive 14 goals in 36 appearances. It was a strike rate that he would maintain, for he was a dangerous forward.

Colin was a native of Barugh Green, near Barnsley. He had a trial with Wolves and also signed amateur forms with Rotherham United before joining the Blades in January 1939. Nearly 5ft 11in tall and very strong and very fast, he had a powerful shot with his left foot and was a fine header of the ball.

The *Sheffield Star*, at the beginning of 1940, commented on his rapid progress and the *Telegraph* noted that 'with luck, he would play for England'. He didn't, but he was always a fine player. He spent most of the war as an armourer in the RAF and was a frequent guest player for Notts County. United saw little of him, though he scored a memorable goal in a War Cup semi-final against Aston Villa in 1944 – the match in which Charlie Thompson, the United centre forward, broke his leg.

Colin came back to the Lane in December 1945 and was a member of the team that won the League North championship. Colin was often given the centre forward position over the next few years, and gave many fine displays – although he would rather have played on the wing, where he had more opportunities to use his pace. He will always be remembered for the five goals he scored in two successive games, playing against Franklin, the Stoke and England centre half, and he was the top scorer in the first three post-war seasons.

Preston North End sought his signature in 1950, but Collindridge rejected the move, and it was a chance meeting with the Nottingham Forest trainer that led to a transfer to the City Ground in August 1950 for £12,500. During that season, he was a member of their Third Division championship side and later played for Coventry, Bath City and Arnold St Mary's in the Central Alliance.

Eddie Colquhoun
Central defender, 1968-78

	Appearances	Goals
League	363	21
FA Cup	13	0
FL Cup	20	0
Other	35	2
TOTAL	431	23

Arthur Rowley served just twelve months as the United manager but made several shrewd signings and none more so than when Eddie Colquhoun came to Bramall Lane from West Bromwich Albion in October 1968 for a fee of £27,500. The six-foot, Scottish centre half made his debut at Huddersfield and a week later took over the captaincy from Len Badger. He stayed at the Lane for ten years – five as captain – before moving to the United States.

Colquhoun was born in Prestonpans, a village in East Lothian, in March 1945 and played in Edinburgh junior football with the YMCA and Edinburgh Norton, when he was spotted by Bury's chief Scottish scout, Jimmy Finnigan. He signed professional terms for the Lancashire side early in 1963 and played for Scotland in the same European youth international tournament that year as Len Badger and Bernard Shaw, who were in the English team which won the trophy at Wembley. The Bury manager and centre half was Bob Stokoe, whose rugged displays had served Newcastle United so well, and Colquhoun always acknowledged how much he learned from his boss. Stokoe converted Eddie from a wing half to a central defender or a full-back and he quickly developed into a fast, powerful and reliable defender.

It was our old favourite, Jimmy Hagan, the West Brom manager, who signed Colquhoun for a small fee in February 1967. Eddie was twenty-one and soon established a regular first-team place. The young Scot was unlucky to miss out on Albion's FA Cup triumph in 1968 because of a serious injury at Newcastle in April, and lost his place to John Talbut. It was still rather surprising when he was allowed to move to United, however. His desire for first-team football was no doubt a major influence in his decision and the transfer fee, in October 1968, was probably about £27,500.

The United manager that season was Arthur Rowley and, just one week after signing for the club, Colquhoun was appointed as the team captain. He had had experience of captaincy at Bury and he was one of those players with a tall, commanding presence who looked the part and his consistent displays fully justified his choice for the position. Strong and determined, he grew in stature with United. John Harris, who had stepped back into the team manager's role, commented that Colquhoun had 'acted as a stabilising influence on a young side' and had brought the best out of the others around him.

He led by example and his colleagues often think back to his no-nonsense decision to take

Colquhoun gets in a header against Watford in the final match of the successful 1970/71 promotion campaign.

the team off the pitch when a match in Zambia was getting way out of hand. Strong and brave, he tackled well, had a fine turn of speed and was particularly good in the air, both defensively and also when scoring goals from Alan Woodward's superb corner and free kicks. He had some great battles with 'old style' centre forwards like Andy Lochhead and quickly disillusioned strikers such as Malcolm Macdonald, who might have thought that Colquhoun would be left behind in a trial of speed.

Eddie led the successful United push for promotion in 1971 and was awarded the first of his 9 Scottish caps in 1972. He was unlucky in that his final appearance for his native country was on a bone-hard, frozen pitch, which was not the best surface for a tall defender to perform on. He was consistent and dedicated and Ken Furphy was surely mistaken when Colquhoun was replaced in 1974 as the United captain by Tony Currie in the hope that the responsibility would boost Tony's morale and international career.

The big Scot's last three years at the Lane were inevitably less happy. The dramatic downturn in the club's fortunes following the financially crippling burden that resulted from the building of the South Stand led to relegation and massive problems. Early in 1978, as part of a plan to cut the wages bill, Colquhoun was loaned to Detroit Express and his contract was cancelled at the end of the year. He later played and coached in the United States with the Washington Diplomats before retiring in 1982 and returning to England.

Bill Cook
Right-back, 1912-27

	Appearances	Goals
League	264	0
FA Cup	33	0
FL Cup	-	-
Other	27	0
TOTAL	324	0

Even by the standards of his time, Bill Cook is unusual in that he played 324 senior games for Sheffield United and yet he never scored a single goal and only once did he play anywhere but at right-back. Given an opportunity to score with a penalty kick in 1915, Bill's shot was so feeble that the goalkeeper kicked it contemptuously away. As a youth, his record was no better; the only time a shot of his went through the goal occurred in a match at Newcastle – but the goal posts were on the next pitch.

A native of Usworth in County Durham (Jimmy Hagan came from the same village), Cook was signed in April 1912 from Hebburn Argyle, made his first-team debut and retained his place, after only four outings with the reserves. Given that he made only 21 appearances for the Blades during the four First World War seasons, Cook's number of first-team appearances give some indication of the consistently high standards of his play and he was the only United player to appear in the two FA Cup successes of 1915 and 1925.

Cook was a happy, unconventional character, who was both a contortionist and a comedian with a fund of funny stories; he could always be relied on to bring laughter to the United dressing room, On the field, Bill was as hard as steel, two-footed and could kick a ball at any angle. Never a fast player, he made up for this by tackling, intercepting and covering shrewdly. He was a tactical player and always 'steady' rather than brilliant.

He was given a free transfer in 1929, although his first-team appearances had all but ended soon after the 1925 Cup Final. He then had a short spell as player-manager of Worksop Town. In all those years with United, Cook had continued to live in the North East, but now his playing days were over, he moved to Sheffield, taking a shop and then keeping the George Hotel in Boston Street. He also worked for twenty years at Metro-Vickers. Cook died in Sheffield in May 1974 and his two FA Cup medals can now be seen in United's Hall of Fame.

Albert Cox
Full-back, 1936-52

	Appearances	Goals
League	267	5
FA Cup	25	0
FL Cup	-	-
Other	41	1
TOTAL	333	6

Few full-backs used the sliding tackle to such good effect and with such precision as Albert Cox (although this author does remember Stanley Matthews picking a careful, though seemingly untroubled, path over Albert's flying limbs).

Cox was born in Treeton, a mining village just to the south of Sheffield. He played for Woodhouse Mill Welfare and joined Sheffield United in April 1935, a couple of months before his eighteenth birthday. He made his first-team debut in February 1936, playing at right-back, and a month later was at left-back in the FA Cup semi-final at Molineux, when United defeated Fulham. He became a regular first-team player in 1937 and was a member of the promotion team of 1938/39, proving equally successful in both full-back positions.

No one ever described Cox as a stylish player, but he was very difficult to pass and very quick to recover; he never knew what it was to be beaten and tackled hard and direct and with speed. He was always a great-hearted player, who never let his team mates or his club down and he was deservedly popular with United supporters.

The Second World War tore a great hole in his football career, although he did fit in some soccer in Egypt playing with Tom Finney for The Wanderers, a Services team put together to entertain the troops. He returned to England in 1943, playing a few games for United and also for Fulham, and then served in France and Germany.

When First Division football began again after the war, Shimwell and Cox were the United backs but after Shimwell was transferred to Blackpool, Albert formed a long and sound full-back partnership with Fred Furniss which, in essence, lasted until 1952. He had two seasons with Halifax Town and later joined the United coaching staff before taking a pub at Woodhouse and a general store in his home village of Treeton – although Coxy's heart was never far from Bramall Lane and he acted as a scout for John Harris for several years.

Tony Currie
Midfielder, 1968-76

	Appearances	Goals
League	313	54
FA Cup	11	2
FL Cup	22	3
Other	30	8
TOTAL	376	67

In any list of outstanding United players of the past sixty years, Tony Currie would feature in the top ten, and only, I suspect, Jimmy Hagan or Joe Shaw might be preferred to head the list, by those United supporters who watched all three in action

Tony was born on New Year's Day 1950 in Edgeware in North London. Tony was on the books of Queens Park Rangers as a boy, but failed to impress and had no better luck when he had a trial with Chelsea. His breakthrough came with Watford, playing as a striker, and it was from the Hertfordshire club that United signed him in February 1968. Tony had won his first England youth international cap in January, but United had noted his promise earlier and an agreement had been reached that Currie would join United for £26,500 when Watford were knocked out of the FA Cup – by coincidence, it was the Blades who were their conquerors in that competition. Currie's value had risen since the agreement was made but Watford's chairman, to his credit, stood by his word.

Currie signed for United at the beginning of February 1968 and made two appearances for the England youth team before making his League debut for United in a First Division match at the Lane against Spurs, when he scored with a header, United winning 3-2. The Blades were engaged in a relegation battle and it seemed that Currie's presence would turn the tide, but not one of the last six home fixtures were won. United returned to the top flight in 1971. By then, Currie was at his brilliant best; an effective, constructive inside forward with dazzling skills and a great entertainer and he could also put away some outstanding goals with powerful shots, though he was not an instinctive goal-scorer.

Currie was special: his ball control was first class and, with the ball at his feet and on the move, his great strength made him a very difficult player to dispossess. His passing, both long and short, was accurate and shrewd. Bubbling with self confidence when he was fully fit and things were going well, his play could be ostentatious and theatrical, dribbling with arms raised, saluting the delighted fans with waves or blown kisses.

No player is beyond criticism. There were some people connected with the Football Association, and within our club, who disliked such extravagances and accusations were made that Tony was a poor trainer, which he denied. Ken Furphy informed the United directors that Currie failed to follow instructions – Freeman said the same thing about Hagan – and yet it

Eddie Colquhoun, Tony Currie and Bill Dearden.

was Furphy who appointed Currie as United's captain in place of Eddie Colquhoun. The reason given to the board of directors by Furphy, was that he believed that the additional responsibility would add something extra to a player of massive talents and help Currie's international prospects. Less than twelve months later, Keith Eddy took over the position of skipper.

Unitedites can only be thankful that they saw Currie at his brilliant best, though his soccer career was far from over when he was transferred to Leeds United (for a £245,000 fee) in June 1976 after the Blades had been relegated and were in serious financial difficulties. Tony won ten more full international caps with Leeds, to add to the seven he had won with United, before joining QPR in 1979. Rangers, then in the old Second Division and managed by Terry Venables, fought their way through to the FA Cup final in 1982, where their opponents were Tottenham Hotspur. The first match was drawn but Rangers, captained by Currie in the absence of Glenn Roeder, were defeated in the replay.

Tony had longstanding injury problems and these became much worse. He was transferred to the Vancouver Whitecaps (£40,000) and then played in Toronto. He returned to England and played non-contract for Chesham, Southend United, Torquay United, Hendon, Dunstable and Goole and then had a period out of the game. These were difficult times, but he returned to Sheffield where, with the help of so many friends and admirers, a successful benefit at the Lane was arranged and his work with Football in the Community has enabled him to pass on his skills and enthusiasm for the game.

Brian Deane
Striker, 1988-93 and 1997-98

	Appearances	Goals
League	221	93
FA Cup	25	11
FL Cup	20	13
Other	7	2
TOTAL	273	119

Brian Deane is a tall rangy striker with surprisingly fine ball control for such a big man. He packs a powerful shot with both feet and is a fine header of the ball. He is one of a small number of players who have had two spells with United and a third has often been anticipated.

His parents had come from Nevis (one of the Leeward Islands in the Caribbean) to Leeds in the 1950s and Brian, the youngest of their six children, was born in the city in February 1968. Turned down as a schoolboy by Leeds United, Barnsley, Notts County and Bradford City, Deane became a part-time player with Doncaster Rovers – where his play was described by a coach as like watching Bambi on ice. However, as his weight and strength increased, he began to look a little more impressive. He made his first-team debut for Doncaster Rovers in February 1986 in a Third Division game against Swansea City.

After 66 League appearances with Doncaster and 12 goals, he was signed by Sheffield United's manager, Dave Bassett after a tip-off from Dave Cusack, who had coached Brian at Doncaster. Few Doncaster supporters regarded the £40,000 fee as a bargain for Sheffield, but they were wrong. Deane was an immediate success, forming a dynamic striking partnership with Tony Agana that took the Blades from the former Third Division to the First in successive seasons.

Deane scored on his debut for the Blades and kept on scoring. Standing at 6ft 3in, with size twelve boots, he was an impressive figure. His ball control, for such a tall man, was remarkable, his heading was excellent and his shooting dynamic. He was undeniably powerful, but many critics thought he needed to be more aggressive. At the Lane, he found the perfect partner in Tony Agana, who had tremendous pace. They scored 46 goals in the League in that first season and both recorded hat-tricks in a 6-0 victory against Chester, Brian scoring a further 21 as United powered their way from the Second Division into the First.

Immediate relegation seemed certain after a dreadful start to the 1990/91 season, but United survived. Brian's 13 League goals proved to be vital and the big striker was awarded the first of his 3 England caps in New Zealand in 1991. The 1991/92 season was again a difficult one for United and Deane. He was injured and he seemed out of sorts when he returned and it was some time before

The life of a modern professional player. Brian Deane and Colin Hill with a young mascot.

it was discovered that he was suffering from an illness. Brian and United recovered, and he recorded another 12 League goals.

In August 1992, Brian secured a permanent place in the history of English League football by scoring the first Premier League goal and the first penalty kick in a match at the Lane against Manchester United. It was the season when United and Wednesday met in a FA Cup semi-final at Wembley and Brian had scored 19 goals in the League and two main cup competitions. However, at the end of that season, with Bassett out of the country, Deane was transferred to Leeds United, earning the Blades over £2.6 million. When he found out about the move, Bassett told the chairman that United would be relegated and, sadly, he was correct.

Deane won a League Cup runners-up medal in 1996, only to return to Bramall Lane in July 1997, asking that he be used only as a striker. Nigel Spackman had taken the role of caretaker manager and had been authorized to sign Deane, paying perhaps about £1m. It was a move which was hugely popular, for 'Deano' was a great favourite with the fans (and rightly so), but the club was in a state of turmoil – and not just in matters of finance – and in January, Deane moved to Portugal, joining Benfica. Soon afterwards, Spackman resigned.

Deane returned to Britain to sign for Middlesbrough in 1998 and has helped the Boro cling on to their Premier League place, although a regular first-team spot became less frequent and his appearances were usually more on the flanks than in his old role as a striker. In November 2001, he was transferred for a nominal sum, rejoining his former boss, Dave Bassett, at Leicester City.

37

Bill Dearden
Centre forward, 1970-75

	Appearances	Goals
League	175	61
FA Cup	7	2
FL Cup	15	5
Other	14	4
TOTAL	211	72

The 1969/70 season was drawing uneventfully to a close at Bramall Lane when the *Sheffield Telegraph* reported that the Blades had signed Bill Dearden, an outside right from Chester, for £10,000, to 'add strength to the club's first-team pool'. The news was not the sort to set the pulses racing.

Dearden, who was born in Oldham in February 1944, had first played as a part-timer for Oldham Athletic, but had been given a free transfer and signed for Crewe before joining Chester in 1968 for a reported fee of £3,000. He was twenty-six when he joined United and had scored 31 goals in 167 League matches. Bill had suffered with cartilage problems, but he was fast and could finish, and he was determined to show that he could offer far more than the sum of his achievements so far. Those who had written him off in the past would be proved wrong.

His first appearances for United were in a County Cup match at the Lane and in Gerry Young's benefit match against the Owls towards the end of April 1970. When the new season began, United seemed to have lost the fluent attacking football which had been a feature of the previous campaign. Dearden made a couple of substitute appearances in Watney Cup games, but the change in his and United's fortunes came with a decision by John Harris, United's manager, to play Dearden at centre forward. This move, coinciding with the return to the team of John Tudor, set United off on a run which ended in a return to the First Division.

Dearden proved to be a dangerous striker because he could use his speed to lose his marker and move into goal-scoring positions and he finished well with both head and feet. He also proved to be a player of real determination and courage – until promotion was secured, United kept it a secret that he had only trained two days a week and had been playing with a cartilage injury.

Bill scored 14 League goals that season and was United's leading scorer in the first two seasons in the top flight. Injuries and age inevitably took the edge off his game, however, and he moved out on loan in February 1976 to Chester and then joined them on a free transfer. He joined Chesterfield in 1977 and became a member of their coaching staff two years later. He moved to Mansfield Town in 1983 and acted for a time as caretaker manager. He moved to Port Vale as assistant manager, but returned to Field Mill as manager in 1999.

Ephraim 'Jock' Dodds
Centre forward, 1934-39

	Appearances	Goals
League	178	113
FA Cup	17	10
FL Cup	-	-
Other	8	5
TOTAL	203	128

The official records fail to reveal the full story of this dangerous centre forward, for the Second World War intervened when Dodds was about to burst onto the scene of the old First Division. By then, he had left United, where he had been our leading goal-scorer for five successive seasons, and had joined Blackpool, but his goal-scoring record with both clubs serve to remind us of a great centre forward.

Dodds was born in Scotland in September 1915, but moved to Leadgate (County Durham) when he was twelve and, from then on, would always be known as 'Jock'. He joined Huddersfield Town when he was sixteen, but was given a free transfer after a couple of seasons. He was snapped up by United, who had just dropped into the Second Division. United had spotted his raw potential and he was soon given an opportunity in the first team, playing at inside left. He did quite well, but then had another spell with the reserves, working hard in training and returning in the afternoons – in particular, to improve his left foot. As a trainer later remarked, 'he could hardly stand on his left leg, let alone shoot with it.'

United needed a centre forward and Dodds was given a chance with the first team. He felt happier but United weren't satisfied until, in his fourth appearance, he scored four goals and never really looked back. In the following season, the Blades had a long undefeated run that carried them through to a Wembley meeting with Arsenal and almost brought promotion; the goals had flowed from Dodds' head and feet.

'Jock' was an irrepressible character with a powerful physique. He was surprisingly fast for his bulk and, in the words of a famous England centre half, he provided 'ninety minutes of rumbustious fun', leaving you 'leg weary, breathless and not a little bruised.'

United had rejected advances from at least seven clubs for Dodds, but he asked for a transfer and, in March 1939, was sold to Blackpool for £10,000 (which was a record for both clubs). The intervention of the war inevitably changed the rest of his career. Dodds set all sorts of records in those seven wartime seasons. Serving in the RAF as a physical training instructor, 'Jock' scored over 250 goals in seven seasons as Blackpool won three successive championships and the War Cup, and he played with equal success for Scotland, scoring a hat-trick against England.

At the end of the war, Dodds was in dispute with Blackpool and played for Shamrock Rovers. He later turned out for Everton and Lincoln City. Dodds was later involved in the 'Bogata Affair' and this brought his direct involvement in the game to an end.

Jimmy Dunne
Centre forward, 1926-33

	Appearances	Goals
League	173	143
FA Cup	10	11
FL Cup	-	-
Other	7	13
TOTAL	190	167

There can be no doubt that Jimmy Dunne was an outstanding centre forward. His goal-scoring achievements for United between 1929 and 1933 are remarkable and his contemporaries heaped praise on him – but there is still much to puzzle at in the playing career of this great Irish player, who holds the United records for the highest number of goals scored in one season and the best ratio of goals per game.

Jimmy was born in September 1905 and played Gaelic football as a boy in Ireland, but switched to soccer and is supposed to have perfected his skills in that game in an internment camp during the time of the Irish Civil War. The validity of such reports is uncertain, but he certainly joined Shamrock Rovers in 1923 and, two years later, New Brighton, the English Third Division team. A little over three months later, having scored seven goals in ten League and cup games, he was on his way to Bramall Lane in exchange for a cheque for £500 – although he needed a good deal of persuasion to sign, fearing that he didn't have the talent to shine in the English First Division.

Dunne was a quiet, modest twenty-year old, and his first three years in Sheffield did little to dispel his foreboding for, as the 1928/29 season drew to a close, he had made just ten appearances in the first team and had scored just one goal. He was not without encouragement, in particular from United's captain, Billy Gillespie, who was a fellow Irishman, and Jimmy had played quite well in the Central League and once for Ireland (not that he was a great success, for he was sea-sick on the way over and was far from well on the day of the game). Appendicitis in 1928 held him back further and the outlook for the young man was far from promising as 1929 dawned.

Seemingly, Dunne's career all turned on two games. The first was a Monday evening fixture at Fratton Park towards the end of April. Pompey had just returned defeated from their first Wembley Cup Final and probably had little stomach for the match. That was of no concern to Dunne, who scored a couple of goals. The new season opened with Harry Johnson, United's record goal-scorer, back at centre forward, and Harry scored in both games, but both ended in defeat. United made changes and gave Dunne another chance and he bagged a hat-trick. His football, reported the *Sheffield Independent*, 'was a revelation'.

From then on, the goals flowed. In the four seasons from 1929/30 onwards, Dunne scored (in the League and FA Cup): 38 in 41 appearances, 46 in 45, 35 in 39 and 28 in 42. He recorded four goals on three occasions in the League and added another four in a County Cup tie against the Owls. He once scored nine-

A United team at Villa Park in October 1932. Front row, third from left: Jimmy Dunne.

teen goals in twelve successive League games; he failed to score in the next match, but added four more in the subsequent two.

Dunne wasn't a big man, but he had all the attributes of a great striker. Jimmy Seed, the Wednesday captain, described him as an 'ideal centre forward'. He had ball control, speed and a great shot with both feet and was too quick-thinking for most centre halves. He could generate terrific power with his head and many of his goals in his first two great seasons came from the fine centres of Fred Tunstall, United's veteran international winger. Indeed, the headline 'Tunnie-Dunnit' became a standard in the Sheffield newspapers as Tunstall, time after time, picked out the fair-haired Dunne and sent across one of his hard and accurate centres; there were many who thought that Jimmy was the best of the lot as far as heading was concerned.

Dunne was sold to the Arsenal at the end of September in 1933. The loss was virtually inevitable. The economic depression in the early 1930s hit Sheffield hard and United were in dire financial straits. They had resisted overtures from several clubs but Herbert Chapman, the famous Arsenal manager, was persistent. Dunne had refused to join the Highbury club in 1932, but this time, Chapman was more persuasive, United accepting an offer of £8,250.

Dunne was only moderately successful with Arsenal and was unfortunate in that Chapman died three months after his transfer. United tried to bring him back to the Lane early in 1935, only to find that he had a cartilage injury and, a few days later, 'Jock' Dodds scored four goals and United's search for a centre forward was over. Dunne was sold by the Arsenal to Southampton in 1936 and, a year later, returned to Shamrock Rovers, first as a player and then as a coach.

Dunne won 22 Irish international caps. There could have been several more, but he often chose to play for United instead. He was only forty-four when he died in his native Dublin in 1949 and his gravestone carries a photograph of this fine player in United's colours.

Keith Eddy
Midfielder, 1972-76

	Appearances	Goals
League	114	16
FA Cup	5	1
FL Cup	6	3
Other	11	1
TOTAL	136	21

It took a little time before Eddy won over his critics at Bramall Lane, but he proved to be a fine midfield player, a shrewd tactician and an excellent captain and United undoubtedly suffered when he moved to the United States in 1976.

He was born in Barrow-in-Furness in October 1944, and was educated at the local grammar school. He became a professional with Barrow, who were then playing in the Football League, when he was eighteen and soon held down a regular first-team place. Ken Furphy, the manager of nearby Workington, spotted his potential, and when the future United manager took over at Watford, Eddy was one of his first signings. Eddy captained Watford when they won promotion to the former Second Division in 1969 and reached the semi-final stage of the FA Cup. Furphy moved on to manage Blackburn Rovers and Watford, with little money available to strengthen the side, were relegated and sold Eddy to United for £50,000.

His debut for United was unusual in that he scored with his first kick. The circumstances were less than remarkable in that United, faced with a penalty shoot-out against Bristol Rovers in a Watney Cup final brought Eddy off the substitutes' bench to take one of the kicks. Keith had a fine record from the spot and this proved to be a problem for some supporters later that season when the new man was selected to take the penalty kicks ahead of Alan Woodward.

Furphy became United's manager late in 1973 and made Currie the captain but, less than a year later, Eddy took the post and earned the respect of the players. He was a calm and commanding player who distributed the ball shrewdly and accurately. Above all, like every fine player, he had the ability to read the game, anticipating the moves of his opponents and possessing the gift of finding space and time before releasing the ball. He could be described as a natural captain, seemingly able to dictate the pace and direction of the game, playing with calm authority and he was 'a good talker', on and off the field, coaxing, challenging and encouraging.

His final season was a disaster for the club. The South Stand was opened but United's financial commitments were crippling and relegation soon became a certainty. Furphy was sacked and became the coach of the New York Cosmos and, in January 1976, Eddy joined his old boss, later playing and coaching in Canada before moving to Tulsa. John Hassall, the United chairman in 1976, remarked that Eddy's departure 'was a great loss to the club'. It was soon obvious that he was correct.

Keith Edwards
Centre forward, 1976-78 and 1981-86

	Appearances	Goals
League	261	143
FA Cup	19	10
FL Cup	17	10
Other	13	8
TOTAL	310	171

Keith Edwards was a master craftsman in the art of scoring goals and a source of delight to United's supporters, for he played with skill, style and artistry – using the rapier rather than the broadsword. He was a fine player and might have been a true great, but we will never know, for he was never tested at the top level of English football.

Born in Stockton on Tees in July 1957, he had an unsuccessful trial with Middlesbrough, playing as a wing half, but was spotted by United when playing for a youth club team. He had a trial, scoring twice for a United reserve eleven in August 1975, and was signed soon after by the United manager, Ken Furphy (who within weeks was sacked).

Keith made his first-team debut that season in an FA Cup-tie at Leicester and also made one substitute and two full appearances in First Division games, but it was a disastrous year for the Blades and, although none could have foreseen it, Edwards would never appear at the top level of English football again.

It was not until March 1977 that Edwards secured a permanent first-team place, but his striking ability was obvious when he scored eleven goals in eight successive League games and he was top scorer that season. It was not an easy time for a young player, however, as United, managed by Jimmy Sirrel and then by Harry Haslam, struggled in the old Second Division. Haslam, always a 'wheeler-dealer', resisted an offer of £30,000 for Edwards from Blackburn Rovers in June 1978, before selling him to Hull City (for between £50,000 and 55,000) early in August.

United sank into the Fourth Division, but in September 1981, Ian Porterfield, the new manager, persuaded Edwards to return to the Lane. The fee, which was fixed by a tribunal at £100,000, was a bargain, for 'King Edwards' set up United's post-war scoring record for a single season with 35 League goals in 41 appearances. Two years later, he scored 33 goals in 44 League appearances and 41 League and cup goals in total and became second in line behind Alan Woodward in the club's post-war list of leading scorers.

Edwards made goal-scoring an art. He certainly couldn't fall back on height or strength and his shooting relied more on accuracy than power, though it was crisp enough. He had confidence in his ability and he would admit that, near goal, he was 'a bit greedy and selfish'. He was quick in thought and deed, with good ball control, adept at finding space with fine anticipation and he was a clinical finisher, with two good feet and excellent heading ability.

Joe Bolton looks on as Edwards attacks the Oxford United goal in March 1985, in his second spell with the Blades.

His work rate was always queried and he was 'not the most enthusiastic trainer'. Another striker said of Edwards, 'he doesn't do a great deal, but around the box, he's deadly'. He would have scored more goals for United if he had taken penalty kicks – and he earned many during his career with his deft footwork and ability to move across a defender and invite a trip – and more of the free kicks. Porterfield also insisted that he took most of the corner kicks and, excellent as they were, most fans felt that Keith would have been better in the middle.

The relationship between Porterfield and the player was never comfortable and was soured by a mean contract dispute but, although he had spells when goals ceased to flow, they never lasted long. He lost form early in the 1982/83 season but returned, scoring a hat-trick after coming on as a substitute against Grimsby. A four-goal haul on the opening day of the 1983/84 season was repeated on one other occasions during that campaign in a Cup-tie at Wrexham. This was also the season in which he scored a a goal of amazing self-confidence against Bristol Rovers, allowing the ball to run through his legs before rounding the 'keeper to score.

His final two seasons at the Lane provided little pleasure for Edwards or the supporters. Injuries were a problem and his relationship with Billy McEwan, who replaced Porterfield as manager, was not harmonious and he was sold to Leeds United in August 1986 for £125,000. Leeds reached the FA Cup semi-final and Edwards scored, but it was a poor season by his standards and he moved a year later to Aberdeen for £60,000, only to return to Hull City in March of the following year. He later played for Stockport County, Huddersfield Town and Plymouth Argyle, as well as non-League with Stafford Rangers and Alfreton Town.

Keith was never a man to hide his opinions and he has, in recent years, offered shrewd comments on United's games for the BBC on local radio.

Bob Evans
Outside left, 1908-1918

	Appearances	Goals
League	204	38
FA Cup	12	0
FL Cup	-	-
Other	4	1
TOTAL	220	39

Bob Evans will always have a place in the history of football, for he is one of that rare breed of men who have won international caps for two nations. Evans is a Welsh name and Bob had a Welsh accent (and always regarded himself as Welsh), but he was capped 10 times by Wales and on 4 occasions by England.

Evans lived as a boy in the Saltney district of Chester on the Welsh side of the river Dee and played for local clubs before joining Wrexham in 1905. His talent was obvious and, during that first season, he made three appearances in the Welsh international team – on the first two occasions as a Wrexham player and the third after he had been transferred to Aston Villa.

United paid £1,100 for Evans and another forward called Kyle, although the bulk of the fee was for the Welsh international. He was tall for a winger with a long stride and could centre well and shoot from a narrow angle. There are contradictions in descriptions of his approach to the game: the Sheffield journalist who wrote in 1914 that Evans 'should go in more and not make arriving a second too late a sort of science', was unlikely to be the one who had earlier written of Bob that he was 'aggressive'.

Evans had won 10 Welsh caps (4 with the Blades) when John Nicholson, the United secretary, discovered that Bob had been born in Chester and his family had moved over the river into Wales when he was three weeks old. The Welsh and English Football Associations were informed and the Welsh were incensed when Evans was chosen for an English international trial and, later that season, played for England in the three home internationals.

Bob earned one further English cap and was the United outside left when the Blades defeated Chelsea in the Cup Final of 1915. During the First World War, Evans worked as a carpenter, playing in local football and making occasional appearances for Tranmere Rovers. He turned up unexpectedly in Sheffield in December 1918 and played in the two Christmas derby matches against the Wednesday but, a few days later, playing in a works' match near his home in Wales, he broke his leg, ending any hopes that he might play again for United.

45

John Flynn
Central defender, 1969-78

	Appearances	Goals
League	190	8
FA Cup	6	0
FL Cup	15	0
Other	20	2
TOTAL	231	10

There is not a great deal in the way of glamour about the town of Workington in Cumbria where John Flynn was born in 1948, and it could be said that this staunch and determined central defender played in similar fashion. Essentially left-footed, he and Eddie Colquhoun formed a hard, determined centre of the defence in the highly entertaining United team of the early 1970s.

Flynn signed for Workington in 1967 and was still a seventeen-year-old amateur when he made his first-team debut. He became a professional only to find at the end of the season that he had been put on the free transfer list. John negotiated a move to South Africa, but a car accident put that on hold and a new Workington manager offered him a contract for the 1968/69 season. It was then that he was spotted by John Harris who, for that season, was working as the general manager of United.

John joined United from his hometown club in July 1969 for a fee of £5,000. He was the last of a very impressive list of players signed by manager Arthur Rowley, but before the new League season had got underway, Rowley was sacked. Flynn had played in two pre-season games in Europe, but his League debut didn't come until November, when he deputised for David Powell. More first-team opportunities came, as Powell proved to be prone to injury.

In the promotion season of 1970/71, Flynn began at left-back, but his most successful and memorable period with the Blades began when he played in the final vital seven matches of that season, none of which were lost and in which he played with the courage and determination which were such a feature of his play.

Strong and quick to tackle and excellent in the air, Flynn, on the left side of defence, with the equally hard and determined Eddie Colquhoun by his side, formed a rock-like centre to the United defence and they were both dangerous targets for Woodward's superb corner and free kicks.

The 1975/76 season proved to be disastrous for United and the fact that Flynn dislocated his shoulder during the second match was a contributing factor. He moved to Millmoor in 1978 and later played with Spalding and, in more recent years, worked for the probation and community services.

Alex Forbes
Centre forward/left half, 1944-48

	Appearances	Goals
League	61	6
FA Cup	9	0
FL Cup	-	-
Other	54	11
TOTAL	124	17

A letter from an unknown correspondent arrived at Bramall Lane in the summer of 1944, recommending a goalkeeper. Teddy Davison, the United manager, replied that we didn't need a goalkeeper, but added as an afterthought, 'Do you know of a good centre forward?' Alex Forbes duly arrived at Bramall Lane with his boots wrapped in a brown paper parcel. Nobody from Sheffield United had ever seen him play. He wasn't a very good forward, but he became one of Scotland's greatest left halves.

Forbes was fit and strong, but had failed his medical for entry into the Armed Forces. He was nineteen and an all-round athlete: he was a fine swimmer but was particularly keen to make a career as an ice hockey player and had been playing football for Dundee North End and had had a trial with Aberdeen. United gave him a match with the reserves and then a first-team debut against Barnsley. He had plenty of dash and spirit and some skill but looked very 'raw'. He scored six goals in his first eight games, but had only added two more when the season ended.

United won the League North Championship at the end of the 1945/46 season and Forbes had excelled, but not as a centre forward. He was making no progress and wanted to return to Scotland, but in November he was given an opportunity at left half. He was naturally right-footed and had never played at half-back, but he made the position his own, frequently training in the afternoon and perfecting his skills.

His red hair, fiery temper, seemingly limitless energy and strong tackling (that was razor sharp) meant that he soon made his presence felt in the First Division, and attracted attention. As a consequence, he had to learn to curb his temper and tackle with more discretion. His anticipation was excellent, his distribution of the ball was first class, he was good in the air and a bundle of energy, and it was no surprise when he was awarded his first cap for Scotland against England in April 1947. He went on to win four more with United and fourteen in all.

He was ambitious and asked for a transfer, being sold to the Arsenal in February 1948 for £16,000. He played for the Championship-winning team that season and was an FA Cup winner in 1950. He played in the Cup Final in 1952 and won a Championship medal in 1953. Cartilage problems ended his playing career at Highbury and he had short spells with Leyton Orient, Fulham, Guilford, Gravesend and Sligo before emigrating to South Africa.

Bill Foulke
1894-1904

	Appearances	Goals
League	299	0
FA Cup	41	0
FL Cup	-	-
Other	12	0
TOTAL	352	0

Bill Foulke will always remain one of the most celebrated goalkeepers of all time and has become a legendary figure in the history of football. What I have called 'Foulke tales' have become part and parcel of the story of our great game, but some are unlikely and most have grown with the telling.

The confusion begins with his name, for at the height of his fame, more often than not, in newspapers and in programmes he is referred to as Foulkes. It is, however, Foulk on the birth certificate – although that may have been a clerical error – and Foulkes on the death certificate. Bill himself thought that Foulke was correct, but he soon gave up trying to persuade United and most journalists to drop the letter 's'.

He was born in Shropshire in 1874, but grew up in Blackwell in Derbyshire, working at the local colliery and playing for the village football team. His talents attracted the attentions of both Derby County and Nottingham Forest, but United made what was probably a more extravagant offer and secured his services towards the end of April 1894, and he stepped straight into the first team when the new season began. There was never any doubt from the very first that United had found a top-class goalkeeper.

It wasn't long before the football world became aware that Billy Foulke was something more than a big, strong man and a good goalkeeper. There has to be another ingredient in a great player. There was, and Bill had it to excess. He was a showman, a character and had a powerful personality – although towards the end of his career, the showman threatened to dominate the footballer.

He was indeed a big man. At 6ft 2in (in an age when six feet was regarded as extremely tall), he tended to dwarf his contemporaries. He was the centre of attention and he knew it, particularly when United were playing away. One of his first acts would be to pick the ball up with one hand and hurl it towards, and occasionally over, the halfway line. His kicking could be prodigious and, on more than one occasion, he fisted the ball into the opponent's half.

In those days, 'keepers were charged vigorously and Bill was the biggest challenge of them all. He was a jovial man with a rather simple sense of humour, who generally accepted these buffetings with aplomb – in any case, it was usually the opponent who ended the floor. Occasionally, however, the big man saw red and opponents were flattened. Opposition fans also sometimes annoyed him and he received warnings that he must not leap over the barriers in pursuit of some unfortunate supporters of the opposition.

Inevitably, stories of Bill's misdemeanours have been exaggerated. One of the most frequently quoted is that Bill picked up Allen, the Liverpool forward, and stood him on his head. Contemporary reports suggest that Foulke dodged aside as Allen charged but couldn't resist bringing him down. The referee claimed that Bill got hold of the player by the arm and the leg and lifted him clean off the ground, and gave a penalty. On another occasion, Bill contrived to collapse on top of Bell, an Everton forward who had charged him once too often; Bell was then picked up with one hand by his jersey collar and handed over on the touch-line to the trainer for repairs.

It is Bill's weight, of course, that grabs the attention. He weighed 14st 12lb in January 1895, but his weight had grown to over 16st by 1898, when United won the League Championship, and was about 19st when the Blades first won the FA Cup in 1899. Later in that same year, he had shed half a stone but he was certainly over 20st when he appeared in the Cup Finals of 1901 and 1902. A 'twenty stone goalkeeper' is the stuff of headlines and his weight had risen to over 22st when he joined Chelsea in 1904.

Legend has it that Bill ended his days in poverty with a penny sideshow at Blackpool, challenging the public to score goals against him. This is not true. He had a shop and a pub in Sheffield, enjoyed racing and was quite a dapper man about town. He died in a local nursing home in May 1916 at the age of forty-two. It is difficult today to imagine how a man who we would regard as 'unfit' could be a successful goalkeeper. The game was different in those days of course; forwards were not as fast and 'keepers made

Bill played four matches for Derbyshire.

more clearances with their feet than today.

Foulke's height, strength and bulk presented problems to opponents and we must accept the contemporary reports which comment on his astonishing agility for such a big man. In the end, we turn to his record. The medals, his England cap and the statistics show that, in comparison to the other 'keepers of the time, he was always one of the very best.

Fred Furniss
Right-back, 1941-55

	Appearances	Goals
League	279	14
FA Cup	24	0
FL Cup	-	-
Other	130	4
TOTAL	433	18

Few United footballers have made their senior debut in such unusual circumstances as Fred Furniss. The match in question was against Everton in May 1941 at Goodison Park and was played out against a background noise of air-raid sirens and anti-aircraft gunfire.

Furniss was born in Sheffield in July 1922 and played for Sheffield and Yorkshire boys and Woodbourn Alliance as a right-back. When his schooldays were over, Fred played for Hampton's Sports at right-back or on the wing, and then played for Fulwood who, in the early years of the war, served as a United nursery side, with Harold Brook and Denis Thompson among their regular players.

Furniss played at right-back with Fulwood and, except for a few rare outings on the wing, that became his position for the remainder of his career. He signed amateur forms for United in 1941 and was given that first senior opportunity at Goodison. He worked as a Bevin Boy in a local colliery and then joined the Army and secured a regular first-team place in October 1943. United had developed a fine crop of young players and many of them played in the League North championship side of 1945/46. Furniss played consistently well at right-back after the war and was a member of the 1952/53 Second Division championship team. It was not until 1955 that he surrendered that first-team place to Cec Coldwell.

Fred was much faster than the great majority of full-backs of his era and was able to attack and support his forwards in a way that we now associate with 'wing-backs', but which was most unusual in those days. He also had an excellent record with penalty kicks, missing just one of the seventeen he took in Football League fixtures.

He joined Chesterfield in 1955, playing with and coaching the reserves, and then played for Worksop, but this most competitive of sportsmen continued to play in local football until he was fifty-five and then refereed Sunday games for youngsters and continued to support the Blades with absolutely wholehearted enthusiasm.

Paul Garner
Defender/midfielder, 1975-84

	Appearances	Goals
League	251	7
FA Cup	14	1
FL Cup	9	0
Other	27	3
TOTAL	301	11

Paul Garner had his ups and downs at Bramall Lane, but was always popular with the supporters. Born in Edlington, near Doncaster, in December 1955, Paul joined Huddersfield Town in 1971 and signed professional forms in December 1972, when he was seventeen. He played in the last two games of the 1972/73 season and became the regular left-back – but this was a dark and difficult period for the West Yorkshire club. Paul appeared in the 1974 FA Youth Cup final, was an England youth international and had made nearly 100 League appearances when United took him on a month's loan in November 1975.

Huddersfield had by then dropped into the Fourth Division and therefore an opportunity to join United in the old First Division, albeit at the bottom, inevitably looked a promising move – no one at that time could have guessed that United would also sink to the lowest level of the Football League. Jimmy Sirrel had just taken over the manager's position at the Lane and Paul was his first signing, United paying £59,555 to secure the young left-back.

United were relegated at the end of that 1975/76 season, but Paul did offer hope for the future. He was of less-than-average height, but always played with refreshing enthusiasm, tackling keenly and using his speed to good effect. Besides being particularly quick in recovery, he was always available to attack with zest down the left flank. Fate took a hand in his career, however, when he was severely injured in a car accident towards the end of August 1977 and he missed the remainder of that season. Later, other severe injuries, which included broken ribs, hindered his development.

Paul was a member of the team that lost to Walsall and dropped into the Fourth Division. He made 34 appearances in Ian Porterfield's championship side, but relations between the two men were never entirely happy. He had a loan spell with Gillingham in September 1983 and, twelve months later, moved on a free transfer to Mansfield Town, where he was in the same Freight Rover Trophy winning team as Tony Kenworthy.

Brian Gayle
Central defender, 1991-96

	Appearances	Goals
League	117	9
FA Cup	10	1
FL Cup	9	0
Other	1	1
TOTAL	137	11

Brian Gayle was a big man who looked the part for a central defender, but he was also big in heart and spirit. He captained United during some difficult times, leading by example so that others couldn't help but follow and it was sad, both for the player and the club, that injury problems restricted his appearances.

He was born in Kingston in March 1965 and was an apprentice with Wimbledon and then a member of the team, managed by Dave Bassett, which was promoted to the First Division in 1986. He made 100 appearances for the Dons in the various League and Cup competitions, but he didn't feature in the FA Cup final of 1988 and joined Manchester City for £325,000 two months later. City secured promotion at the end of his first season but, when Howard Kendall became the manager at Maine Road, Brian was sold to Ipswich for a similar amount in January 1990.

United reported the signing of Brian from Ipswich early in September 1991, but there were financial difficulties under the chairmanship of Paul Woolhouse and it was not until Bassett intervened with a personal loan of £100,000 that the transfer was completed. The quoted fee of £750,000 was a record for United, who were at the bottom of the table.

Bassett needed to stiffen the defence, but he also had lost Vinnie Jones and Bob Booker had finally run out of steam. Brian Gayle had the qualities of leadership and determined fighting spirit that were required, and he not only steadied the defence but took over the captaincy, and United gradually recovered and finished ninth. Brian was a big, powerful man and very good in the air – he scored two goals with headers at Maine Road that season and also earned a footnote in history by scoring the own goal of the season when an inadvertent header looped over Mel Rees and secured the championship for Leeds United.

Gayle captained United in the new Premier League and he led the team out at Wembley in the FA Cup semi-final, but injuries meant that he could only make 13 League appearances in the 1993/94 season when United were cruelly relegated, and another injury at the end of the following season ended play-off hopes.

The spirit was willing but an arthritic knee problem brought top-class football to an end. He made a sentimental final appearance for United in the last match of the 1995/96 season against Port Vale and then moved to Exeter City on a free transfer. He signed for Rotherham United in October, had a loan spell with Bristol Rovers and later played for Shrewsbury, Kettering Town and Telford.

Billy Gillespie
Inside left, 1911-31

	Appearances	Goals
League	448	127
FA Cup	44	10
FL Cup	-	-
Other	71	24
TOTAL	563	161

Billy Gillespie will always be remembered as one of United's and Ireland's greatest players and captains. For his country, he established records for both appearances and goals: he scored the goals when Ireland defeated England for the first time and played for Ireland when they first succeeded in winning the home international championship and he played for his country over a period of seventeen years. For United, he led the team to the club's fourth FA Cup triumph and also the semi-final stage in 1923 and 1928, and only Jack Pickering played for United for a longer period.

He was born in Kerrykeel in County Donegal in August 1891. He played his first serious football in nearby Londonderry as an amateur with Derry Institute and Derry Celtic and was about to sign for Linfield when he was persuaded to become a professional with Leeds City – the forerunners of Leeds United – in May 1910. United paid £500 for him in the week before Christmas 1911. He was then regarded as a 'striker' with a good goal-scoring record and he did well with United and was unlucky, because of a broken leg in the first match of the 1914/15 season, to miss out on United's FA Cup triumph against Chelsea in the so called 'Khaki Final'.

His first Irish cap came in February 1913, when Billy scored both Irish goals in what was his country's first victory over England. He played a massive part in the following season when Ireland won the home international championship for the first time, scoring both Ireland's goals in defeating Wales and also scoring in a remarkable 3-0 victory against England at Middlesbrough. He was eventually capped 25 times by Ireland and scored 13 goals (and there were at least eight occasions when he was chosen by his country but elected to play for United).

Gillespie returned from active service in the First World War, having by then lost most of his hair and playing as a more constructive inside forward. He had fine ball control, a natural body swerve and never lost his shooting ability and, although he was never fast, his long raking stride was deceptive and took him away from many an opponent. His balding head was a delight to the many soccer caricaturists of the day and that is how he will always be remembered. He was a master strategist and constructive player and his passing, both long and short, was both shrewd and accurate. He was a master of the long cross-field ball, switching the point of attack; this ploy had been a feature of United's successful teams since the

Gillespie greets the Glasgow Association captain in a match at Bramall Lane.

mid-1890s and that tradition was carried on by Jack Pickering in the 1930s after Gillespie had retired.

Like Jimmy Hagan, 'Gilly', as he was known by his colleagues, disliked heading the ball and when he had little option but to do so, it was known to draw a cry from the John Street terrace on the lines of, 'Don't do that, lad. It'll spoil thy parting.'

Gillespie took over the captaincy of United in 1923. Billy was a great strategist and thought deeply about the game but was, according to some of his playing colleagues, not as fine a captain as Utley. Gillespie was essentially a quiet man who out-thought his opponents, whereas Utley was more demonstrative and out-fought them – but it was a matter of opinion. Harry Johnson declared that Gillespie was 'the best captain one could play under'. Jack Pickering, a future United international inside forward who was groomed by the Blades to take over from Gillespie when the great man retired, was terrified, in his early days, of making a mistake and hearing Gillespie's growl of displeasure in the tones of a sergeant-major, saying 'he made sure you remembered your mistakes.'

Gillespie last played for United in August 1931 at Blackpool, when he was nearly forty. He coached the new 'A' (third) team for a while and then, in June, 1932, became the manager of Derry City. He returned to Sheffield during the last war and died in Bexley (Kent) in 1981, aged eighty-nine. He was a great footballer by any standards and a man who loved the great game.

Harold Gough
Goalkeeper, 1913-24

	Appearances	Goals
League	242	0
FA Cup	19	0
FL Cup	-	-
Other	74	0
TOTAL	335	0

Harold Gough made a decision in 1924 to secure his future and probably spent the better part of the rest of his life regretting it, for his decision to become a pub landlord wrecked his football career. Less than a year later, he was behind the bar of the Railway Hotel in Castleford and Charles Sutcliffe, a moderate Third Division goalkeeper from Rotherham United, was standing beneath the United bar at Wembley with an FA Cup winner's medal in his sights.

Born in Chesterfield in December 1890, Gough joined Bradford Park Avenue in 1910 and made three first-team appearances for the Second Division side before joining Castleford, who were members of the Midland League. He signed for United towards the end of April 1913. Gough then had a great stroke of fortune as the first-team 'keeper, Ted Hufton, broke his nose. Gough seized the opportunity and seven months later appeared in the FA Cup semi-final and then was a member of the team that defeated Chelsea in the 1915 Cup Final.

Gough was described as both 'brilliant and reliable' and allowed nothing to worry him. He was physically very strong, punching with power and could kick the ball over the halfway line with both feet and 'if he was coming out for a ball, it was his.' He worked at Fryston Colliery during the early part of the First World War and then served in the Navy and was an occasional guest player for Leeds City and Hibernian. He played for England against Scotland in 1920, though he was not at his best, playing with a bruised hand, and toured South Africa with the FA that summer. A more serious injury meant that he played no part in the FA Cup run of 1923 when United reached the semi-final, but his playing career all but collapsed when, in the summer of 1924, he took the hotel in Castleford.

Gough claimed that he was unaware that he was breaking the conditions of his contract with United, though it was clearly stated that the player was 'not to engage in any business which the Directors might deem unsuitable' and in essence, this meant licensed premises. True or not, he assumed that United would continue to employ him or place him on the transfer list, but he hadn't reckoned that the matter would be placed in the hands of the Football Association, who cancelled his player registration. This was restored in January 1925 but, tied to living in Castleford and with a high League transfer fee on his head, his football future was bleak.

Gough played again for Castleford and then Harrogate Town, but it was not until early in 1927, when his transfer fee was cut to £500, that he was able to return to the Football League, playing for short periods with Oldham Athletic and Bolton Wanderers and then, two seasons with Torquay United, before an injury brought his playing days to a close. He returned to Castleford and died there in 1970.

Colin Grainger
Outside left, 1953-58

	Appearances	Goals
League	88	26
FA Cup	7	1
FL Cup	-	-
Other	3	0
TOTAL	98	27

You are very fortunate when you see an outstanding footballer at his best. Some, like Jimmy Hagan, go on and on but there are others, who, for a variety of reasons, shine like a brilliant star and then, all too soon, show they are mere mortals. Bramall Lane saw such a player when Colin Grainger was at his peak.

Born in June 1933, Colin was a native of Havercroft, near Wakefield, and was a younger brother of Jack Grainger, Rotherham United's powerful outside right. A cousin played for Wrexham and Colin joined their groundstaff, but National Service in the south of England delayed his progress and he had only 5 League appearances to his credit by the time he joined United in the close season of 1953.

The United manager, Reg Freeman, had been well aware of Colin's potential. Grainger was twenty and undoubtedly fast, but he had a much lighter frame than his brother and gave little indication in that first season, when he had 3 League outings, that he had much of a future in the game. Grainger was in his second season when Freeman gave the young player an extended run in the first team.

Colin was stronger and fitter by this time and though his first four games were defeats for United, Freeman persisted. It was reported that Colin could 'do even time on the track' and it began to show. Sadly for United, Freeman died at the end of that season and his successor, Joe Mercer, was unable to prevent United returning to the Second Division. Mercer's coaching and advice was sound, however, and his position in the game was also no doubt helpful in advancing Grainger's course. Colin played for the Football League and then made his England debut at Wembley against Brazil, scoring twice. He earned five more caps with United.

He was now at his brilliant best and very difficult to stop, for he was tremendously fast with good ball control and he left most backs in his wake, passing them on either side. He could put across good centres and was dangerous cutting in, for he shot well and was a good header of the ball. In reality, he was often stopped of course – Second Division full-backs, with flying elbows or outstretched legs, frequently brought him down and referees seemingly only acted when the damage was done. There were too many injuries and they included a serious one sustained when playing against Wales.

He was sold to Sunderland in 1957 – winning one further cap – but the Wearside club were in a turmoil and were relegated in the following season. He had a season with Leeds United, which was no more fruitful, before moving on to Port Vale, Doncaster and Macclesfield Town. He played over 300 League games in all, but undoubtedly, those at the Lane were the best.

George Green
Left half, 1923-34

	Appearances	Goals
League	393	10
FA Cup	29	0
FL Cup	-	-
Other	16	0
TOTAL	438	10

In his later years at the Lane, it was suggested in the press that George Green should be known as 'Honest George', such was his reputation within the club and with its supporters. Green had been a splendid international left half and was a member of the 1925 Cup-winning team. George was born in Leamington in 1901 and worked as an apprentice turner and fitter. He was playing for Nuneaton Borough when United signed him in 1923. John Nicholson, the United secretary, later wrote that the transfer 'was secured under rather peculiar circumstances' but neither Green or Nicholson (to the author's knowledge) ever explained the mystery.

George came to United as a right half who had also played at right-back and on the right wing, but he was asked during a preseason practice match to switch to left half and play behind the left-wing duo of Gillespie and Tunstall. In Green's words, 'We struck up an understanding almost straightway' and the three players became one of the most famous and feared 'triangles' in the game. Signed during the close season, Green, in his new role as a left half, was plunged immediately into first-team duties and he had a memorable debut, for the match was Manchester City's first fixture at the new Maine Road ground, with 57,000 spectators in attendance.

Green's place in the United eleven was secure for many seasons. He was a member of the 1925 FA Cup-winning side and won the first of his eight caps in 1926. He was a strong player and a fine tackler and his passing, normally on the floor with the side of his foot, was crisp and accurate. He had the ability to disguise his intentions, 'feinting to do the obvious and achieving something entirely different by lightning speed of motion and high skill'. Above all, he was consistent and reliable: it was part of his make-up to never appear excited but always pegging away. He certainly never lacked courage and determination. During a famous home defeat by Blackburn Rovers, which eventually ended 5-7, Green dislocated his shoulder but it was put back without any anaesthetic and he came back on and played until the final whistle. George was an all-round sportsman and a violinist, which earned him the nickname 'Fiddler' from his colleagues.

He took over the captaincy in 1931, but the severe economic depression of the early 1930s hit United hard and they were relegated for the first time in their history at the end of his final season at the Lane. He became the player-manager of Leamington Town and then a publican. He died in March 1980.

Jimmy Hagan
Inside forward, 1938-57

	Appearances	Goals
League	361	117
FA Cup	28	5
FL Cup	-	-
Other	53	29
TOTAL	442	151

There can be no doubt that Jimmy Hagan was the most skilled and entertaining Sheffield United player of all times; he was probably our greatest ever player in the very widest sense, although Ernest Needham, who led the United side in the golden years at the turn of the century, may have been more influential. Words, however, are a poor substitute for memory, and those readers who remember Hagan will treasure the joy of recalling a brilliant football artist of rare genius.

Hagan, the son of a former professional player, was born in High Usworth, County Durham in January 1918 and was a schoolboy international. He joined Liverpool when he was fourteen, but the Football League ruled that he was too young to be on their ground staff and he returned home. A few months later, League regulations forgotten, he joined Derby County. Jimmy made his first-team debut in December 1935, but first-team opportunities were slim with County, for they had an all-international forward line, and so he agreed to join United in November 1938 for a transfer fee of £2,925 and played an influential part in the successful drive for promotion in 1939.

War service, mainly as a physical training instructor in England, gave Hagan greater strength and weight and these factors, added to his brilliant ball skills, led to a regular place in the excellent wartime England team. Jimmy made 16 appearance for England and only Raich Carter and Tommy Lawton scored more goals for England in wartime internationals. He also made over 90 war appearances for Aldershot, one for Huddersfield Town and (perhaps) one for Shrewsbury Town.

He returned to the Lane early in 1946, when United won the League North championship, but the insecurity of football led Hagan to refuse United's terms when peace-time soccer resumed, although a solution was found when he became, for a time, a part-time player. When he was a part-timer, Jimmy trained for the most part with the 'A' team players in the evening but not, according to one fellow part-timer, if it rained – 'Jimmy changed but got straight in the bath'. He was fit, however, and opponents were mistaken if they thought a hard man would stifle his genius. There was a sensation at the Lane when Hagan was sent off in a match against Swansea Town. Hagan was cautioned but not suspended.

He was capped again in 1948 against Denmark and was a member of FA touring teams to Canada and Australia and represented the Football League, but he was otherwise ignored by the England selectors in spite of almost perpetual arguments in his favour in the national press. Frank Swift, the England goalkeeper said of Hagan that 'the record books make a mockery of his ability'.

Jimmy captained United for three seasons,

Hagan shakes hands with King George VI before a wartime international at Wembley.

but relinquished the position after relegation in 1949, only taking up the role again for one other season. In February 1951, Wednesday offered a British record £32,500 for Hagan, but the player refused to move and said he would finish his career at Bramall Lane.

Hagan was a remarkably consistent player and had the good fortune to miss few games because of injury. Dark-haired, about 5ft 9in tall and weighing about 11st, he was the perfect inside forward, equally at home on the left or right side of the field. He never regarded himself as a fast player, but was quick enough and his football brain was super fast – certainly too much for opponents but also occasionally for his colleagues. His ball control was perfect, he was two-footed and could shoot with both power and accuracy. He had a trick for every circumstance and was very difficult to tackle or dispossess and for twenty years, his wonderful skills provided a feast for United's supporters and never more so than in his ability to collect a high ball and instantly wheel away in one sweet movement as though, in the words of Joe Mercer, he had 'a claw in his boot'.

No player is perfect. Reg Freeman, the United manager, said of Hagan, 'at team talks, he agrees politely and then ignores it all on Saturday'. Hagan could certainly be stubborn and idiosyncratic. He was a quiet, reserved man with a dry sense of wit. He was good company with the friends he knew but he would never sell himself. Hagan could head a ball but it certainly wasn't a major part of his game. He took a few penalties, but probably missed as many as he scored and some of his colleagues – while full of admiration for his talents and completely willing to admit that the fortunes of the team depended so much on Hagan's ability – would, nevertheless, wish at times for a more orthodox and straightforward partner.

The quality of his play remained high to the very end: he was thirty-nine when Liverpool came to the Lane in April 1957, desperately seeking points for promotion, and yet Hagan destroyed them and the crowd rose to him as he left the field with a tumult of appreciation. Hagan's last first-team appearance for United was at Derby on the 14 September, 1957.

Hagan's first managerial post was at Peterborough. He took them into the Football League, where they scored a record 134 goals. He then moved to The Hawthorns and also managed Benfica and Sporting Lisbon. He died in Sheffield in February 1998.

Hagan, summing up his playing days, said, 'Every game has been an outstanding memory. I love to play.' We were so fortunate to see this man: such skill and talent are rare and to be in the presence of genius is to be blessed.

Derek Hawksworth
Forward, 1950-58

	Appearances	Goals
League	255	88
FA Cup	17	6
FL Cup	-	-
Other	14	9
TOTAL	286	103

All managers make mistakes and Teddy Davison was no exception, but the signing, late in his career at the Lane, of the two wingers, Alf Ringstead and Derek Hawksworth, was a masterstroke and the two players, together with Jimmy Hagan, Len Browning and Harold Brook, formed an exciting and dangerous forward line.

Derek Hawksworth was born in Bradford in July 1927. He could and did play in all of the forward positions, although he was essentially a right-footed player. He had played for Bradford Park Avenue during the war as an amateur, and after service in the RAF in India, he signed for Huddersfield Town, but only became a professional when David Steele, who had been the manager at Park Avenue but was now at Valley Parade, signed him for Bradford City.

Sheffield United paid £12,500 for him – a record for City – and he made his debut for the Blades at outside left, a fortnight after right winger Alf Ringstead's first appearance. Both players scored in that match and the two dangerous wide men were to play an important role when United, managed by Reg Freeman, captured the Second Division championship in 1953.

A strong forceful player and difficult to knock off the ball, Hawksworth could use his pace to advantage down the wing, usually putting across dangerous crosses, but he could also cut in to great effect as he had a powerful shot. He was also a good header of the ball and could take knocks. As a result of this, although at first he played mainly at outside left – and that was his best position – from about 1955, he frequently featured at centre forward and was in effect used as a utility forward, playing in any position on the forward line. He was chosen for the Football Association against the Army in November 1951 and, at the end of that season, played for England 'B' against France.

Hawksworth was transferred in May 1958 to Huddersfield Town in an exchange deal for Ronnie Simpson and £6,000. David Steele signed him for a third time when he moved to Lincoln City, but Derek moved back to Bradford City in January 1961 and then played for Nelson, before opening a newspaper shop in his native city.

Ted Hemsley
Midfielder/left-back, 1968-77

	Appearances	Goals
League	247	7
FA Cup	11	0
FL Cup	17	2
Other	18	1
TOTAL	293	10

Ted Hemsley may be remembered as the player who missed the vital penalty kick in the Watney Cup final of 1972, but that was a minor blemish in the career of one of the most reliable, committed and consistent United left full-backs. His tackling was strong and decisive, he was very difficult to pass and his covering and marking were excellent. He was the Supporters' Club Player of the Year in 1973 and will also, probably, prove to be the last of our players who was also a county cricketer.

Hemsley was born in Stoke in September 1943, but brought up in Shropshire. It was while he was at Bridgnorth Grammar School that he was spotted by the Shrewsbury Town player-manager, Arthur Rowley. Ted was given his first-team debut when he was seventeen and eventually captained the team, chalking up 235 League appearances. When Rowley came to Bramall Lane in 1968 as team manager, with John Harris taking a new position of general manager, Hemsley was the first player he signed.

Hemsley, purchased as a tough tackling midfield player, struggled to establish a regular place in the side and his position may have appeared even less secure when Rowley was sacked. However, in November 1969, he was given an opportunity at left-back, taking the place of Mick Heaton, and he never looked back.

The team were rapidly growing in confidence and finally achieved promotion to the old First Division in 1971. Ted held his first-team place until 1975, when a stomach injury led to the introduction of Paul Garner into the side. Ted was given a free transfer in 1977 and ended his soccer career with a spell with Doncaster Rovers. He continued to play cricket for Worcestershire until 1982 and also ran a turf accountant's business in Dronfield for many years.

Billy Hendry
Centre half, 1891-95

	Appearances	Goals
League	69	2
FA Cup	8	0
FL Cup	-	-
Other	44	1
TOTAL	121	3

Only nine years after Sheffield United Football Club came into being, the Championship was won and, twelve months later, the FA Cup. It was a remarkable achievement and yet Billy Hendry, the Scottish player who laid the foundations for those triumphs, remains largely unknown.

Hendry was probably born in Dundee, though Newport, on the other side of the river Tay, is another possibility. He played football for Dundee Wanderers and then, like so many of his countrymen, crossed the border into England to become a professional player. He was a talented forward and played for West Bromwich Albion in the first Football League season of 1888/89, and then played for Stoke before returning to Dundee. He then went south again to play for Preston North End – the team that had won the first two League Championships.

It was Charles Stokes, the United chairman, who secured Hendry's transfer and made him the team captain. Hendry was now playing at centre half, although the position was less defensive in those days. Stokes had signed a fine player, but of far greater significance was the fact that United had found a player with the quality, leadership and know-how that would bring a more professional attitude within the club.

He was a stocky player, who was neat, scientific, cool and effective 'with fine ball control; an artist who headed the ball superbly'. He was later described, by a United colleague, as 'the best player Sheffield ever had'. He was also a natural leader on the field and, in those days of course, a captain's role within the club was far more senior than it is today. A local journalist wrote of Hendry that United placed their confidence in him 'both as to the arrangement and formation of the team. The club relied on his ability as a player, as a captain and as an adviser.'

Under his leadership, United secured a place in the First Division and the foundations were laid for the great team at the close of the century. It was also said that it was Hendry's advice and guidance that brought the natural genius and talents of Ernest Needham to the perfection that he would soon display. Hendry's career with United essentially ended with an injury in his native Scotland in Leith on New Years Day 1895 and the first benefit match arranged for a United player took place at Bramall Lane, later that season, on his behalf. He later played for Dundee, Bury, West Herts (Watford), Brighton United and, lastly, Shrewsbury, where he died in May 1901.

Trevor Hockey
Left half, 1971-72

	Appearances	Goals
League	68	4
FA Cup	1	0
FL Cup	9	0
Other	4	0
TOTAL	82	4

New blood, whether in the form of a player or manager, can often revitalize a team's fortunes. Trevor Hockey provided an excellent example of this when he joined United towards the end of January in 1971. He will be recalled when other players who made far more appearances are but shadowy figures of the past.

United lay fifth in the former Second Division table and the story of the previous season was being repeated. The players had ability and attacked with style, but disappointing away results and a lack of steel in the centre of the park were a threat to hopes of promotion. United turned to the transfer market, exchanging John Tudor for John Hope and David Ford and paying a transfer fee of £40,000 for Trevor Hockey. Hope's signing was significant, for he played splendidly in goal that season, but the critical signing was that of Hockey.

Hockey's Welsh father had moved to Keighley to play rugby league and Trevor was born there in May 1943. He joined Bradford City as a schoolboy and made his debut when he was sixteen. Small but determined, his energetic displays on the right wing attracted the attentions of Nottingham Forest and he moved there in November 1961 for a record City fee of £15,000. Two years later, he joined Newcastle United for £25,000 and was a member of their 1964/65 Second Division Championship side, only to move yet again in November 1965 to Birmingham for a similar figure. His six seasons in the Second Division at St Andrews was his only stay of length in what was a nomadic career. Trevor had played as a wing forward, but developed with Birmingham into an ebullient and aggressive wing half.

There can be no doubt that his energetic displays played a large part in United's successful promotion bid. He was vocal and demonstrative, but he followed his manager's instructions – which were to battle, win the ball and give it to Currie. With his distinctive beard and wearing a headband, when in the right mood he was an inspirational player and thoroughly deserved his 9 Welsh caps.

All three of his final games in December 1972 were lost, and he was dropped and asked for a transfer. He moved to Norwich City in February 1973 in an exchange deal with Jim Bone. At the end of that season, he joined Aston Villa and a year later returned to Bradford City. He was the player-manager of Athlone Town and manager of Stalybridge Celtic and also played in the United States, but died in Keighley in April 1987 at the early age of forty three.

Glyn Hodges
Midfielder, 1991-96

	Appearances	Goals
League	147	19
FA Cup	16	3
FL Cup	7	0
Other	1	0
TOTAL	171	22

It is rare to read an article about Glyn Hodges, an attacking left-side midfield player who won 18 full Welsh caps (five of them with United), where he is not described as 'enigmatic'. Dave Bassett, who was his manager over so many years, noted that it was 'stupid for a player of his talent to have achieved so little'.

Glyn was born in Streatham in April 1963. He joined Wimbledon as a schoolboy and, a year after becoming an apprentice, he made his League debut in September 1980 in a Fourth Division game at Halifax. He took part in the rousing campaigns that saw the Dons rise from the Fourth to the First Division, winning a Fourth Division championship medal in 1983 and becoming Wimbledon's first international in 1984 when he came on as a substitute for Wales against Norway.

He was transferred to Newcastle United in July 1987 for £300,000, but after only eighty-nine days on Tyneside, Dave Bassett, his former Wimbledon manager, who had moved to Watford, signed him for the Hertfordshire club for £250,000. Bassett then became the manager of Sheffield United and tried to sign Hodges in the 1990 close season, but Glyn chose to stay in the London area, joining Crystal Palace.

Early in 1991, United, facing almost certain relegation from the First Division, took Hodges on loan and his fine play and vital goals helped preserve the club's place in the top flight and his permanent transfer was secured for £410,000 in mid-April. He continued to delight – and infuriate – the crowds at the Lane until he was given a free transfer by Howard Kendall in February 1996, when he joined Derby County and played a small part, mainly as a substitute, when they won promotion that season. He played for a while in Hong Kong and then returned to Britain and, after trials with Nottingham Forest and Chesterfield, joined Hull City in August 1997. February 1998 saw him return to the City Ground and, eleven months later, he played for Scarborough. He joined the coaching staff at the Lane in February 2000 and then moved to Oakwell.

Hodges always was a player of moods. Mainly left-footed, his play could both delight and frustrate. Talented and stylish to a degree, but totally unpredictable, he often lacked 'application, concentration and tolerance', was 'his own worst enemy' and (yes) invariably 'enigmatic'.

Alan Hodgkinson
Goalkeeper, 1954-71

	Appearances	Goals
League	576	0
FA Cup	52	0
FL Cup	24	0
Other	23	0
TOTAL	675	0

Joe Shaw is the only United player to have played more games for the club than Alan Hodgkinson, whose playing career spanned three decades. Although Alan was rather small for a goalkeeper – his height was a little over 5ft 9in – his agility, consistency and almost faultless technique, remarkable judgement and anticipation, quickly brought him to the attention of the England selectors.

Alan was born in August 1936 in Laughton en le Morthen in South Yorkshire, but his childhood was spent in nearby Thurcroft and he left school to start his first job as a butcher's boy. He had played for Worksop Town as a fifteen-year-old in the tough Midland League, making his debut at Halifax. Huddersfield Town expressed an interest in the youngster, but didn't pursue the matter and so Reg Freeman, the United manager, stepped in and secured a gentleman's agreement with Fred Morris, the Worksop manager, that Alan could have a trial with the United reserve side when he was sixteen, with United paying £250 to Worksop if the player joined the Blades on his seventeenth birthday. Freeman was shrewd enough to disguise his keen desire to secure Hodgkinson by showing an apparent greater interest in another Worksop player.

Alan's early ability was quite remarkable. He played for the 'A' team and then for the reserves against Bury in April 1953 and his first-team debut was an away match in August 1954 in a First Division match against Newcastle United, which the Blades won 2-1. He gained a great deal of experience with Army and representative sides while serving in the Royal Signals during his National Service. This complicated his appearances for United and his first game for the England under-23 team was sandwiched between appearances in the United third eleven. He appeared in the full England side in that same season, with only 30 League and cup appearances under his belt and, because of Services commitments, he didn't become a regular first-team player until January 1956.

The United 'keeper in the early 1950s was Ted Burgin, and Alan learned a lot from that extremely fit, agile and brilliant player and they would return on many an afternoon to the gym or the old bowling green on Cherry Street to perfect their skills. However, the newcomer had no intention of being a carbon copy of his mentor and they were, in any case, very different in temperament.

Alan will always be remembered as the 'keeper in the fine United defence that first came together in September 1957. In front of Hodgkinson were full-backs Cec Coldwell and Graham Shaw and half-backs Brian Richardson, Joe Shaw and Gerry Summers. The six players suffered few injuries and made a final appearance together in August 1963. They are best remembered for the 1960/61 season, when United were promoted to the First Division and had three hard-fought cup semi-final battles with Leicester

The defence: Alan Hodgkinson; Cec Coldwell, Graham Shaw; Brian Richardson, Joe Shaw, Gerry Summers.

City, but they were involved in regular FA Cup campaigns that deserved more success.

Hodgkinson was awarded 5 full caps (and was never on the losing side) and 7 at under-23 level and also played for the Football League. A loyal one-club man, 'Hodgy' made over 650 first-team appearances for Sheffield United and it was only in the final few months of his playing career that his reputation as the most reliable of goalkeepers began to waver. Early in 1971, Alan made way for John Hope in what turned out to be another promotion season for the Blades.

His record with United had been outstanding. In the period between August 1957 and May 1970, he missed just 26 League games and will always be remembered for his dependability, judgement and for having the safest pair of hands in the game – it is difficult to imagine any 'keeper letting through fewer 'soft' goals.

He joined the United coaching staff for a time and later assisted Gerry Summers when he became the manager of Gillingham. Alan then became a specialist goalkeeping coach, eventually concentrating on assisting the Scottish national side and he became a familiar figure, working alongside the Scottish national manager, Craig Brown, finally hanging up his boots and gloves in 1999.

Bill Hodgson
Inside/outside left, 1957-63

	Appearances	Goals
League	152	32
FA Cup	18	1
FL Cup	6	2
Other	7	2
TOTAL	183	37

Billy Hodgson may have been the smallest and most lightweight player in the fine United side of the late 1950s and early '60s, but he lacked nothing in energy and his total commitment and meaningful play, allied to fine ball control, made him a popular and valuable player.

Bill was a Glaswegian, born in July 1935. He played for Dunoon Athletic and then played for St Johnstone, but National Service brought him down to the South Coast of England where he was allowed to assist Guildford. Joe Mercer, the United manager, took him on loan in 1957 and signed him in November, after his seventh first-team appearance, United paying a fee of £3,250.

Although Bill was only 5ft 6in tall, he was a lively character and very tricky. He also proved, in his first season during a Cup-tie against Tottenham at White Hart Lane, that he could do an excellent marking job, snuffing out the threat of Danny Blanchflower as United recorded a famous 3-0 victory. Bill was equally at home on the left wing or as an inside man, but Ronnie Simpson eventually took the wing position with Bill as his inside partner. Hodgson also played at outside right for a time in the promotion campaign of 1960/61, when United also reached the FA Cup semi-final.

His last appearance was against Chelsea in September 1963, when he was injured in a collision with Bonetti, the visitor's goalkeeper, and it was in a sense the end of an era in United's history – for that game was also the last appearance together of the great defence which had battled through so many FA Cup campaigns and taken United back to the First Division.

Bill was transferred to Leicester City for £20,000 and later played for Derby County, Rotherham United and as a player-coach with York City, where he assisted Joe Shaw and acted as caretaker manager when Joe resigned. Bill had a full FA coaching badge and returned to the Lane in 1970 to help with the juniors but, twelve months later, for 'domestic reasons', he returned to Scotland, making a handful of appearances and coaching with Hamilton Academicals.

David Holdsworth
Central defender, 1996-99

	Appearances	Goals
League	93	4
FA Cup	13	3
FL Cup	7	0
Other	5	0
TOTAL	118	7

Howard Kendall, the United manager, invested heavily in new players in 1996 in an attempt to take the club back to the Premier League. David Holdsworth was one of the new men and he brought stability and strength to the defence – it was no fault of his that the gamble failed so narrowly at the end of that season. Holdsworth remained with United, proving to be an excellent central defender and captain, providing calm authority in a period of turmoil within the club.

David and his twin brother, Dean, were born in Walthamstow in November 1968. They signed for Watford, taking the step up from apprentices to full professionals when they were eighteen. Dean was given few opportunities at Vicarage Road and left but David remained, making over 300 appearances in League and cup games. He had captained the England under-17 team and was an England youth and under-21 international.

Holdsworth joined the Blades in October 1996 for a fee of £500,000 and he was an instant success at the Lane, soon taking over the captaincy and forming a fine partnership with Michel Vonk and then with Carl Tiler. Too many points were dropped, however, and United went into the lottery of the play-offs, to be beaten at Wembley by a dramatic last-minute goal.

The following season was one of constant turmoil with changes in the board, coaching staff and an amazing turnover in players. Nigel Spackman, the manager, resigned and Steve Thompson took the caretaker-manager role. Holdsworth remained steadfast and, under his leadership and thanks to his last-minute goal in the FA Cup against Coventry City, the team, against all the odds, reached both the FA Cup semi-final and the play-offs in the League.

The following season was almost as heartrending: Steve Bruce came in as manager and partnered Holdsworth in defence, but David missed four months of the season due to injury. He returned and had lost none of his determination – another vital late FA Cup goal helped take United through to the historic tie at Highbury. United were seventh in the table when the decision was taken in March to accept a bid from Birmingham of £1.2 million for Holdsworth. It was a sad end for a player who deserved better.

He was a first-class central defender, having all the necessary strengths and no significant weaknesses. He was good in the air, comfortable on the ball and he had strength, pace and determination – but he also had those extra qualities that made him a fine captain. He had the ability to lift the other players, to organize a defence, to keep going against the odds and, above all, he was reliable, consistent and one of the most popular players to play for the club.

Harry Hooper
Full-back, 1930-46

	Appearances	Goals
League	269	10
FA Cup	23	1
FL Cup	-	-
Other	15	1
TOTAL	307	12

Harry Hooper was the United right-back and captain when the club lost to the Arsenal in the 1936 FA Cup final. Born in Nelson in Lancashire in 1910, he had joined United in February 1930 from Nelson who, in those days, played in the Football League Third Division (North). He made his first-team debut at the end of that year and established a reasonably permanent place at left- or right-back in 1931. Hooper was two-footed but, from 1934, his regular position was at right-back.

Early in the 1935/36 season, Archie McPherson, the United captain, was dropped from the first team and Hooper took over the captain's role; McPherson subsequently regained his place in the side but Hooper retained the position of skipper in a season when United hit a winning streak which took them to Wembley and all but secured one of the two promotion places. Hooper kept the position of captain until the beginning of the 1937/38 season, when Tom Johnson took over.

Hooper was a smart-looking, well-groomed man – as befits someone trained in his youth as a tailor – with his dark hair always brushed straight back. He was a fine kicker of the ball and put real bite into his tackle, but his greatest strengths were his speed, his shrewd, calm play and, in particular, his ability to keep an opponent on the touchline and out of harm's way.

Hooper had an excellent record with penalty kicks. The first he ever took hit the crossbar but his other ten attempts with the first team were all successful (one of those was stopped by the goalkeeper, but Hooper seized on the rebound and scored). Accuracy was his strength, but they were hit crisply, either side of the 'keeper and usually just inside the post.

Like so many others, Harry lost many of his playing days because of the war. He had missed the end of the promotion season of 1938/39 because of injury and Army service meant that he made less than a handful of appearances for United during the war. He made 9 first-team appearances in the 1945/46 League North championship season and then played regularly in the Central League side before moving on to Hartlepool United in 1947. Later, after the transfer of his son from Birmingham to West Ham United, Harry joined the training staff of the east London club. He returned to Halifax Town as their manager from 1957 to 1962 and died there in 1970.

Rab Howell
Half-back, 1890-98

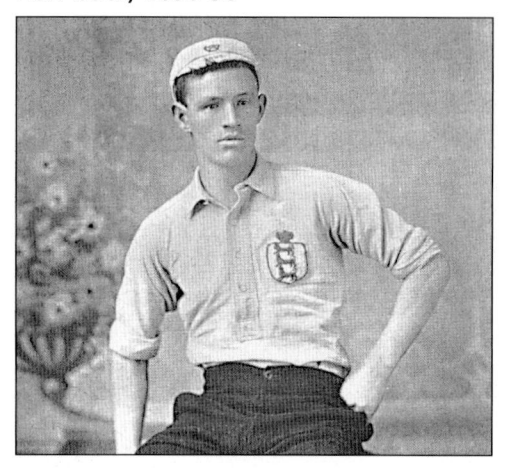

	Appearances	Goals
League	155	6
FA Cup	22	0
FL Cup	-	-
Other	63	5
TOTAL	240	11

It is a sad fact that this fine player, who served United so well from the very first season until the League Championship was almost won, left the club in circumstances which cast a shadow on his reputation. The shadow may be totally unjustified, but it remains and the truth is unlikely to emerge after the passage of so many years.

'Rab' Howell was born in a caravan in the Wincobank district of Sheffield, probably in 1869. His father was a horse dealer who sold pots and pans and 'Rab' was often known as 'The Little Gypsy'. It appears that his name was registered as 'Rabbi' – but this author suspects that this was an unfortunate error on the part of the registrar, who heard the (no doubt illiterate) father murmur a familiar form of Robert.

Howell was one of three fine United players – Watson and Whitham were the others – who had played for Ecclesfield and Rotherham Swifts. All three came to Bramall Lane in March 1890, no doubt tempted by the offer of 10 shillings per week. 'Rab' played at centre forward at first and then centre half, but moved in his second full season to wing half and when United entered the Football League in 1892, he took the right half position with Ernest Needham on the left.

He was a small man (standing at 5ft 5in tall and generally weighing about 9 st) but he certainly punched his weight. Many opponents were frightened by this little player who usually played without stockings and was rarely injured. He was as 'hard as nails', a ball winner, and could reduce an opponent to helplessness, 'sticking to him like a leech'. He was fast, even on heavy ground, and 'terrier-like', although his passing and shooting were less impressive.

Howell was capped twice by England, but off-the-field trouble and 'Rab' ran hand in hand. On at least eight occasions, he informed the United Committee that he 'would mend his ways' and the club gave him extra money to meet the crises that came his way. His leaving the club was, however, a very different kettle of fish. A key game in 1898, as United fought desperately to capture the League championship, was an away fixture at Roker Park. On two occasions, a cross from the Sunderland right passed in front of Foulke in the United goal and appeared to be going out for a goal kick. Both were intercepted by Howell, who was supposedly 'attempting to clear', and entered the United net. Were these unfortunate accidents or something more corrupt? Howell was left out of the challenge match against Celtic and the Dewar Shield match against the Corinthians. He played in the next fixture and was then sold to Liverpool.

He played well with Liverpool and with Preston North End, but his days as a player were ended when he broke a leg in 1903. He died in Preston in 1937.

Tommy Hoyland
Right half, 1949-61

	Appearances	Goals
League	181	12
FA Cup	15	2
FL Cup	2	0
Other	11	4
TOTAL	209	18

Tommy Hoyland is one of that small group of former United players – 'Old Harry' Johnson, Peter Boyle and Colin Morris are others – who had the pleasure of watching a son play in those same red and white stripes. Tommy began as a forward but was more successful when he was moved to right half in the mid-1950s.

A native of Sheffield, Tommy was born in June 1932 and played for Sheffield boys before joining Oaks Fold, a United nursery club. When he was seventeen, he played for a United eleven against the Western Command Army team and, a month later in November 1949, he made his reserve-team debut. He was still only seventeen and playing at outside right, when he was given a first-team opportunity at the Lane in a Second Division match against Leicester City and, cutting in from the wing, scored a fine debut goal.

Any thoughts that this fine start to his career as professional meant that he would have an instant regular first-team position were not borne out by events. Tommy had some injury problems and National Service intervened and it was not until the 1954/55 season that he had a regular first-team spot. It was in that season that he moved to right half, rather than playing at inside right or on the wing. Hoyland was at his best in the mid-1950s as part of a fine half-back line with Joe Shaw in the centre and Jim Iley playing at left half.

Tommy was strong, fast and mobile, quick to join an attack or to get back into a defensive position and he was equally at home in both aspects of the game. He didn't have a reputation for being an aggressive player, but he tackled well and his sending off in a cup replay (in one of many tussles with Dave Hickson of Huddersfield Town) in January 1957 was an isolated incident.

The 1957/58 season proved to be a watershed in his career, for he lost the number four shirt to Brian Richardson. He made a few appearances at inside right and showed that he had lost none of his shooting ability by scoring a hat trick at West Ham and played again at wing half when Richardson was in the Army.

Hoyland finished his League career at Valley Parade, joining the Bradford club in October 1961, for a fee of £6,500. He later played for Retford Town and Alfreton and was a licensee in Sheffield, little more than a stone's throw from the Lane.

Ernest Jackson
Right half, 1933-49

	Appearances	Goals
League	229	7
FA Cup	21	0
FL Cup	-	-
Other	150	12
TOTAL	400	19

Born in June 1914, within a stroll of Bramall Lane in the Heeley district of Sheffield, Jackson played for Sheffield and Yorkshire boys. Although he was a United supporter, Ernest signed amateur forms for Sheffield Wednesday and then had a trial with Grimsby Town, before accepting an offer to become a part-time player earning £1 per week from United in July 1932 and he was still employed at the Atlas & Norfolk works in Sheffield when he made his first-team debut seven months later.

Ernest quickly developed into a fine right half-back and was probably the fittest United player of those days. He had tremendous body strength and he worked hard on developing a long throw. He was a quick and powerful tackler with good ball control and had a fine sense of anticipation and judgement. With his distinctive fair hair and a fresh complexion, he was a conspicuous figure on the field.

A cartilage injury and operation in the spring of 1935 held him back, but he regained his first-team place and, playing better than ever, was a member of the 1936 Cup Final team and among the players who won promotion back to the First Division in 1939. Jackson was frequently referred to as a player who deserved international honours, but the war intervened and the opportunity disappeared.

Jackson returned to his old job during the war and gave up playing for a short time because of the long working hours and travelling difficulties. He was still a fine player in the immediate post-war years, but was released in 1949. Curiously, both his debut and final first-team appearance were against Wolves, but the latter game ended with a crushing 6-0 defeat; Jackson, a man of principle and strong opinions, knew that it was time to go. He had a season as player-coach with Boston United and then became a member of the United training staff. He became the first-team trainer when Reg Freeman succeeded Teddy Davison as manager and they worked well together. The Second Division championship was captured in 1953 but, after Freeman's death in 1955, Ernest couldn't establish a satisfactory working relationship with Joe Mercer, the new manager, and resigned.

After a spell out of the game, he became the trainer of Rotherham United and then moved on to Chesterfield. He died in his native city in 1996.

Harry Johnson (senior)
Right half, 1895-1908

	Appearances	Goals
League	242	6
FA Cup	31	1
FL Cup	-	-
Other	2	0
TOTAL	275	7

The Johnson family from Ecclesfield have played a large part in Sheffield United's past, for Harry Johnson (senior) was a Championship medal winner in 1898, an FA Cup winner in 1899 and 1902 and his two sons, Harry and Tom, brought further honours to the club. 'Young Harry' remains United's record goal-scorer and was an FA Cup winner in 1925, while Tom played in the 1936 Cup Final and captained United's 1938/39 promotion team.

William Harrison Johnson was born in January 1876 and first played for the Norfolk Works and Ecclesfield Church clubs. He had trials with Barnsley, but wasn't impressed with their offer of ten shillings per week and came to Bramall Lane in 1895. He made his League debut for the Blades in the Championship season of 1897/98, making 10 appearances in all and scoring the only goal in a vital home match against Sunderland.

He took Rab Howell's place in the team and soon proved to be a consistent, hardworking right half-back, who never knew when he was beaten. A strong player with tremendous stamina, he could 'play on the heaviest ground without turning a hair, was resolute to a degree, a fair but strenuous player whose heading was almost perfect'. He was a fine tackler, difficult to dispossess and good in the air – always trying to head the ball to United's advantage. Needham, his captain, described Johnson, who had 6 England caps to his name, as 'scrupulously fair, a cheery companion and wonderfully clever'.

Making a rare appearance at full-back in January 1906, a terrible injury all but ended his career; his leg was smashed just above the knee and it was thought that he would never play again. He did, in fact, make a few further appearances in the first team before taking control of the reserves and then, in August 1909, he accepted the position of assistant trainer and also occasionally assisted the groundsman. He remained at the Lane until 1934, known to one and all as 'Old Harry' to differentiate him from his most famous son. He died in Ecclesfield in July 1940.

Harry Johnson
Centre forward, 1916-31

	Appearances	Goals
League	313	201
FA Cup	27	20
FL Cup	-	-
Other	55	31
TOTAL	395	252

United's popular record-scoring centre forward was a son of 'Old Harry' Johnson, the former international right half and assistant trainer. 'Young Harry' was relatively small and slim, very fast with seemingly inexhaustible energy and fearless. He was also a part-time player, working as a metallurgical chemist in a steel works. It was said that he missed more easy goal opportunities than he scored, but his tally of goals was remarkable. He played football with a smile and boundless enthusiasm and, like his father, was an FA Cup winner, leading the United forward line in the 1925 victory at Wembley.

Harry was born in Ecclesfield, a village to the north of Sheffield and the source of so many United players. He was a pupil of Barnsley Grammar School and signed amateur forms for United in 1915 – he would later claim that in a reserve game at Heckmondwike, the home supporters turned hostile and one threatened him with a revolver! He made his first-team debut in March 1916 in a wartime match at Hull and began to hold down a regular first-team spot in 1917, often appearing at outside right or inside forward. He missed most of the 1918/19 season while serving in France. He also made wartime appearances for Notts County (against United), Birmingham and Rotherham County.

His Army service over, he returned to Bramall Lane in the autumn of 1919 and scored 12 goals in 26 League and cup appearances that season and recorded his first hat-trick. Before his days at the Lane came to an end, he would score five goals in one game – a United record he shares with Hammond – and further records in scoring four goals on seven occasions and twelve hat-tricks (one should not forget that seven of these were made before the change in the offside law and that Harry is the only player to record a hat-trick in a United v. Wednesday FA Cup tie).

The new offside law, which was introduced for the 1924/25 season, undoubtedly suited United, and Johnson in particular. It provided more scope for a team that placed greater emphasis on attack than on defence and United scored more goals in that season than any other team in the top two divisions. Forwards had more space, and players with pace were in their element – and this perfectly suited Johnson. Billy Gillespie, United's Irish international inside left, was another to benefit, for he was a master of long, accurate passing; Fred Tunstall, at outside left, thrived on the passes of Gillespie and left half George

The Johnsons: Tom, 'Old Harry' and 'Young Harry'.

Green, and left many an opponent gasping as he raced away to fire across the dangerous centres that provided so many goals for Johnson in the centre; finally, at outside right, the mercurial David Mercer provided crosses of pinpoint accuracy.

Johnson led the United scoring charts for nine successive seasons and was the idol of the fans, both male and female – women had noticed his habit of hitching up his shorts, which were too large for his 'slim, boyish frame', and he was the recipient of a plentiful supply of knicker elastic. Technically, Harry was not a great player. All agreed that he missed more 'sitters' than any other player but 'he was the greatest scorer of impossible goals'. It was his speed, anticipation and courage that brought him those opportunities and he was a fine header of the ball, often flying 'horizontal' through the air. He chased every lost cause and seized on his opponents' errors and confusion. He was difficult to mark and had amazing industry and enthusiasm, explaining that his attitude to the game was due to the fact that he worked during the week, making each game something special to look forward to.

His play was far from perfect and his first touch often let him down (indeed he never properly learned to trap a ball). He was never a schemer or ball player and he had 'off-days' and was dropped – often scoring another hat trick for the reserves. He was cheerful, he was fearless, he 'bounced around as if made of India-rubber' and always came up smiling. In a word, he was a 'trier' – and that was the word he used to describe his play.

His younger brother, Tom, joined United in 1928 but was slow to develop and the two never played together in the first team. Harry had one representative honour, playing for the Football League and scoring three goals, although 'Dixie' Dean of Everton hit four!

He was transferred to Mansfield Town in 1931 for £500, but soon showed he was far from finished by scoring 104 League goals for the Stags and becoming their record goal-scorer. There was an occasion at Mansfield that speaks volumes for this amazing player. He had never been prone to injury – 'if he was hit, he always seemed to be rolling' – but he broke a wrist in 1934. A subsequent X-ray showed six other breaks that had never been reported. He retired from the game in 1936 and died in Sheffield in May 1981.

Tom Johnson
Centre half, 1930-41

	Appearances	Goals
League	183	0
FA Cup	19	0
FL Cup	-	-
Other	55	0
TOTAL	257	0

The Johnson family of Ecclesfield played a massive part in the story of the first fifty years of Sheffield United. Harry Johnson (Senior) was a member of the League Championship side of 1897/98 and the Cup Final teams of 1899, 1901 and 1902, and later became a member of the United training staff. His eldest son became United's record-breaking goal-scorer and played in the 1925 FA Cup final team and Tom, the youngest boy, played for the Blades in the 1936 Cup Final, creating a family record in the great competition that has never been equalled.

It is never easy to become a successful professional footballer. How much harder it must be when your father was an international and your brother has an FA Cup winner's medal and is the idol of the supporters. There was a twelve-year age gap between the brothers. Tom was born in May 1911 and signed for United in 1928, but he was far from impressive in his early years as a part-time professional. Taller and much sturdier than his brother, he played in the reserve team as a defender or wing half, but at the end of the 1933/34 season, when United were relegated for the first time in their history, Tom had made less than 30 first-team appearances, and his application to become a full-time professional was rejected.

United's regular centre half was Jimmy Holmes, a rough and tough player but unhappy with the defensive 'third-back' or 'stopper' centre half position. Johnson worked hard on this more defensive role, but he was dropped once again early in the 1935/36 season. He returned to the first team on Boxing Day 1935 and everything seemed to fall into place, as the team set out on an unbeaten run that carried them through to a Wembley final against Arsenal and narrowly failed to win them promotion. Tom took over the captaincy of the team in 1937 and led United back to the First Division in 1939, playing with 'courage and astonishing strength'. That was a fine side but, sadly, war intervened.

Tom worked as an electrician at Whitwell Colliery and played regularly for United until the close season of 1941. By then, he was in the RAF but was discharged, late in 1943, with an ankle injury. His last game for United had been at Everton in May 1941 – Fred Furniss made his debut in that same match – and he probably never appeared again in our colours, although he was registered as a United player until February 1946. Early in 1946, he signed for Lincoln City and it was with Johnson as their captain that the Imps won the Third Division (North) title in 1948. Tom died in Sheffield in August 1983.

Mick Jones
Centre forward, 1963-67

	Appearances	Goals
League	149	63
FA Cup	11	9
FL Cup	7	1
Other	5	3
TOTAL	172	76

Mick Jones was the centre forward in the young United First Division team of the mid-1960s. The average age of the team was low and they were mainly local players. Their formation and progress was a great achievement for John Harris, the manager, and Archie Clarke, his assistant.

Mick Jones was born in April 1945 in Rhodesia, a hamlet near Worksop, but his family moved when he was three to nearby Shireoaks. He played for Worksop and Nottinghamshire schools and had an unsuccessful trial, when he was fourteen, with West Bromwich Albion. United spotted him when he was playing for Dinnington Miners' Welfare and he was invited to train with United on two evenings a week. Harris was impressed with him in a practice match and he became an apprentice in 1961, scoring freely in the Northern Intermediate League side.

Well-built, determined and hardworking, he made his first-team debut at Old Trafford in April 1963, just four days before his eighteenth birthday, and celebrated his actual birthday with two goals at Maine Road. He formed a very effective dual strike force, at first with Derek Pace and then, in the 1964/65 season, with Alan Birchenall – many hearts were broken at Bramall Lane when the latter pair were sold in 1967.

Jones had a strong shot in both feet, was a fine header of the ball and led his line well, using his strength to hold the ball and distributing it well to supporting players. He was awarded 9 England under-23 caps and 3 full international honours; the first two came in 1965 when he was a United player and the third in 1970.

Jones was sold to Leeds United in September 1967 for £100,000 – a record fee for both clubs – and played an important role in the success of his new club, his direct and powerful approach combining well with the more rapier-like approach of Allan Clarke. Honours that came his way included Championship medals in 1969 and 1974 and a FA Cup winners' medal in 1972, when he dislocated his elbow just at the moment that Clarke scored the winning goal from Mick's centre. A knee injury meant that he played no first-team competitive football after the Championship was won in 1974 and he was forced to retire in August 1975.

Alan Kelly
Goalkeeper, 1992-99

	Appearances	Goals
League	216	0
FA Cup	22	0
FL Cup	15	0
Other	2	0
TOTAL	255	0

Alan Kelly, United's Republic of Ireland goalkeeper, followed in the footsteps of his father, who made 47 appearances for Ireland during the course of a long and distinguished career with Preston North End. Alan's elder brother, Gary, who was also a goalkeeper, started his professional career with Newcastle United but Alan, who was born in Preston in August 1968, joined his father's club at Deepdale. Alan had played as a full-back with Preston Boys and with Preston North End youth teams, only taking over in goal when another player was injured. Kelly trained as an electrician and his progress as a goalkeeper was hampered by a broken leg and head injuries suffered in a traffic accident and then a further break while playing in a testimonial game.

Dave Bassett was the United manager who signed Kelly in August 1992, the initial fee of £150,000 rising to £200,000, and his first full Republic of Ireland cap came six months later. It was a good upward move for the player, who made his League debut against Arsenal, and United never had cause for regrets. Alan proved to be a sound and reliable goalkeeper and a first-class professional, who was universally popular with supporters. He was later quoted in The *Sheffield Telegraph* as saying, 'I loved the club and living in the Peak District. It was a brilliant time in my life.'

For seven years, Kelly and Simon Tracey vied for the first-team goalkeeping place and it was a tribute to both players that they remained good friends. Undoubtedly, the most memorable moments of his period at the Lane were his three penalty shoot-out saves in the FA Cup tie against Coventry City that took United into the 1998 semi-final. Kelly never sought a transfer, but United's financial problems and the fact that Tracey was far more than a capable deputy, led to his transfer to Blackburn Rovers in July 1999 for a £700,000 fee, which included an £80,000 payment to Preston.

Tony Kenworthy
Defender, 1976-86

	Appearances	Goals
League	286	34
FA Cup	17	1
FL Cup	21	1
Other	33	3
TOTAL	357	39

Tony Kenworthy was born in Leeds in October 1958 and his family were Elland Road regulars, but he had a trial at Bramall Lane and became a Sheffield United player. A hard-tackling, essentially left-footed midfield player, he had played for Leeds Boys and had captained the Yorkshire Boys team and made his debut in the United reserve side when he was sixteen. He was still only seventeen when he made his First Division debut at Carrow Road in April 1976, and he became an England youth international later that same year.

Sadly for Tony and the Blades, the final six games of that 1975/76 season in which he appeared were to prove the only occasions when he played at the top level of the Football League. His career at the Lane coincided with many dark days, which included relegation to the Fourth Division, but his fighting displays and one hundred per cent effort always offered encouragement to United fans that brighter times lay ahead.

Tony always had the qualities that supporters require of a player. He played with effort and determination in a no-nonsense style that few opponents relished, and his tackling was incisive with speed and directness. He wasn't tall, but was superb in the air and proved to be an excellent central defender, being equally at home at left-back or at left or right half. He scored some fine goals for United with fiercely-struck free kicks and headers and had an excellent record with penalty kicks. Many fans will remember his two successful penalty kicks in a keenly-fought battle at Tranmere in the Fourth Division championship season of 1981/82 and a headed goal in the umpteenth minute of injury time against Wigan in 1983, when Kenworthy came through a crowded penalty area in a way that brooked no argument.

A fiercely competitive player, Tony came through several operations that threatened to end his career and was rewarded after his transfer to Mansfield Town in 1986 with promotion, and in 1989 by scoring the winning goal for the Stags from the penalty spot in the final of the Freight Rover Trophy.

Keith Kettleborough
Inside forward, 1960-66

	Appearances	Goals
League	154	17
FA Cup	15	4
FL Cup	10	1
Other	4	2
TOTAL	183	24

Keith Kettleborough never pretended to offer the star quality or the artistry of an illustrious inside forward like Jimmy Hagan, but he did an excellent job of work in that difficult position, linking defence to attack and satisfying both departments. He was skilful and industrious, working constantly and effectively like a cog in a well-oiled machine.

Kettleborough, who was an excellent cricketer, was born in Rotherham in June 1935. He was small and slight as a boy and it wasn't until he was serving in the RAF that he began to acquire the body strength and stamina that would serve him so well as a professional footballer. He had a two-week trial with Grimsby Town, but gave up the idea when the club asked him to stay on for a further fortnight, but joined Rotherham United when he was twenty, after playing for the local YMCA.

Keith held a regular place in the Rotherham team from 1957, in a period when both the Blades and the Millers were playing in the former Second Division. It was John Harris who brought Keith to the Lane in December 1960. United led the table but were short of forwards and Willie Hamilton, the brilliant but wayward inside forward, was not playing well. United paid £15,000 for Kettleborough, who made his debut against Bristol Rovers at the Lane. United had played ten home games and won the lot but, on that day, everything turned to ashes for United. The ground was heavy but United and the new player played well and took a two-goal lead, before Bristol fought back and equalized; then Hodgkinson's thumb was broken before a free kick to the visitors took a freak bounce and the game was lost.

Keith went on to play consistently well for United, though he missed much of that promotion season because of injuries. In the autumn of 1963, with United at the top of the table, he was chosen as reserve for a Football League side and called up for training with the England squad, but an injury and cartilage operation wrecked his progress.

He was a fine constructive inside forward, passing the ball simply but effectively and providing the through balls that forwards such as Russell, Pace and Simpson thrived on. He was far from being a robust player in appearance, but he was difficult to knock off the ball and dispossess and there was an aggressive aspect to his play that occasionally brought him to the referee's attention.

Newcastle United paid £22,500 for Kettleborough in January 1966 in a successful bid to escape relegation and he later was the player-manager of Doncaster Rovers, reverting after a short time to the role of player only, and then playing for Chesterfield and Matlock Town.

Joe Kitchen
Forward, 1908-20 and 1920-21

	Appearances	Goals
League	248	105
FA Cup	21	6
FL Cup	-	-
Other	73	58
TOTAL	342	169

Joe Kitchen was the United centre forward in the 1915 Cup Final, scoring the third goal with a typical individual burst. He is one of the few players who have joined the Blades on two separate occasions.

Kitchen was born in Brigg in Lincolnshire in 1890 and made his Football League debut when he was sixteen, playing for Gainsborough Trinity, and was still only seventeen when he made his debut for United in March 1908.

One of his main attributes was a tremendous burst of speed, putting the ball past an opponent on one side and swerving by with long strides on the other and, although he usually featured at centre forward, many thought he was even more dangerous playing at outside right, though it was not a position that he enjoyed. He was 'as hard as nails' and an individualist noted for 'solo dashes', 'electric rushes' and first-time shooting – but his heading was judged to be no better than adequate.

He was near to international selection as early as 1909, but his form dropped away a little. He was back to his best by 1914, when United reached the semi-final stage of the FA Cup and played well in 1915 when United took the trophy for the third time. He lost some of his best years to the First World War and was injured when chosen for two victory internationals in 1919.

In August 1920, after a disagreement over terms, he was transferred to Rotherham County for a substantial fee but he wasn't happy there and returned to Bramall Lane four months later, United agreeing to pay the same price (although the board of directors were not unanimous over the decision). Joe's best days were over and in September 1921, United accepted a fee of £250 from Hull City. He later played for Scunthorpe United, Gainsborough Trinity, Shirebrook and Barton Town where, although a teetotaller and non-smoker, he became the landlord of the Wheatsheaf Hotel.

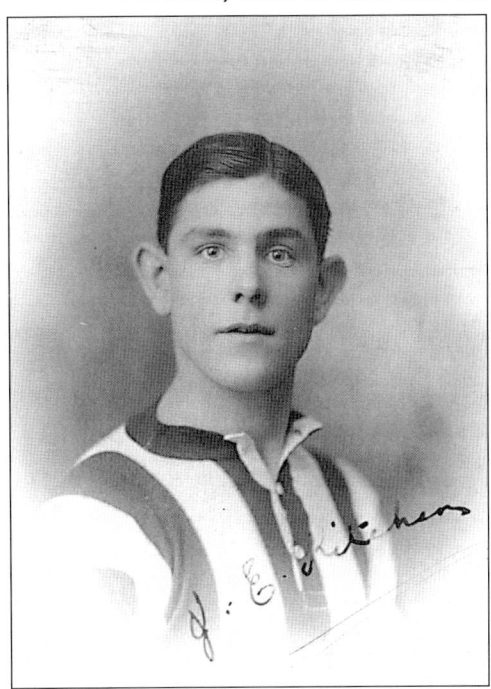

Harry Latham
Full-back/Centre half, 1940-53

	Appearances	Goals
League	190	1
FA Cup	19	0
FL Cup	-	-
Other	218	0
TOTAL	427	1

The term 'stopper centre half' perfectly described Harry Latham, the Sheffield United central defender. Powerful and well-built, good in the air and a determined tackler, there was little that could be called stylish in Harry's play, but he was difficult to pass and never gave less than one hundred per cent.

Latham was born in the Carbrook district of Sheffield in January 1921 and had joined United before the outbreak of the Second World War. Harry and Walter Rickett both made their first-team debut in January 1940 at Rochdale and Latham soon held a regular first-team place, playing at full-back and then at wing half while working as a furnace man. He first moved to centre half in 1945, when Bill Archer missed the Victory Celebration game, and played regularly in that position from November, in the season when United won the Football League North championship. He captained United in 1946, in 1949 and in 1950/51 and made 25 appearances in his final season of 1952/53 – when United won the Second Division championship team – before joining the training staff.

Nicknamed 'Scodger' by the fans and 'Shudder' by his colleagues – 'We should have won, we should have scored' – Harry was a first-rate professional and a good 'club man'. He was a determined player, who didn't like losing – in fact just the type of player that a manager needs on the training ground, in the dressing room and on the pitch, particularly when things aren't going well. Latham could never be considered as an outstanding footballer, but he never gave less than his best. Not surprisingly, he was at his best on the heavy grounds, battling against big, vigorous centre forwards – both of which were a feature of football in those days.

Harry joined the United training staff in 1953 as Ernest Jackson's assistant and took over the first-team job in 1956. He had never been on a coaching course and had not got the confidence, or will, to attend one. Although other people came in and took responsibility for coaching, Harry remained as a valued and popular member of the training staff until 1974. He died in Rotherham in July 1983.

Joe Lievesley
Goalkeeper, 1904-12

	Appearances	Goals
League	278	0
FA Cup	9	0
FL Cup	-	-
Other	1	0
TOTAL	288	0

Joe Lievesley was born in Staveley in North Derbyshire in 1883. It was hardly surprising that when he showed outstanding ability as a young goalkeeper, Sheffield United signed him, for Staveley's most famous inhabitant was United's captain, Ernest Needham. Joe, who incidentally preferred his surname to be spelt 'Leivesley', made his first-team debut in September 1904. He took over the position as United's number one goalkeeper from Bill Foulke in November, beginning a quite remarkable run of appearances that continued until the end of December 1911, during which he missed just six competitive first-team games.

Lievesley was always described as dependable, calm and cool. He never seemed flustered and had none of the flamboyant and showmanlike character of Bill Foulke, his famous predecessor. He was a fine goalkeeper 'who seemed to know exactly what advancing forwards intended to do', and 'made his work look easy'. He was chosen for the England trial match in 1910, during which he saved a penalty kick, and played for the Football League against the Southern League and toured South Africa with the FA in the summer of 1911. His last first-team game for the Blades was at Bramall Lane in October 1912, when he was injured. Joe Mitchell, the reserve goalkeeper who had had few opportunities because Lievesley had been so consistent, took his place – although he in turn was supplanted by the young and brilliant Ted Hufton, who would go on to win international honours with West Ham United.

Lievesley was given a free transfer and joined the Arsenal. He served in the Royal Flying Corps during the First World War and played for Chesterfield Town until the close season of 1917, when the club were closed down by the FA for making illegal payments to their players.

The Lievesleys were a football family: two of Joe's brothers, Fred and Wilf, were professionals, as were three of his sons, including Leslie (who was the Torino coach and perished in the air disaster in 1949). An uncle of his was the international full-back, Harry Lilley, who played for United in the early 1890s.

Joe Lievesley was also a good cricketer and played for Sheffield United and later for Rossington, where he died in October 1941.

Bert Lipsham
Outside left, 1900-08

	Appearances	Goals
League	235	29
FA Cup	24	5
FL Cup	-	-
Other	-	-
TOTAL	259	34

John Nicholson, the United secretary, and Arthur Bingham, a member of the Football Committee, went to Crewe to sign Bert Lipsham, but their initial attempt failed. They did, however, get him to agree to accompany them back to Crewe station and they continued to put forward the benefits of a transfer to United. When they arrived at the station, they had to persuade a member of the staff to delay the departure of their train before finally getting Lipsham to sign the necessary papers.

Herbert Broughall Lipsham had been born in Chester in April 1878 and educated at the King's School. He worked as an accountant in the local office of the Official Receiver, but was also playing as a professional footballer with Crewe Alexandra when he came to United's attention.

Lipsham was an outside left with a long raking stride and a considerable turn of speed. The young player was fortunate in that he played with Ernest Needham, who could feed him with accurate passes and the winger had the skill to take these unhesitatingly in his stride and was noted for his fast – too fast in Needham's judgement – accurate crosses. He had a good shot with both feet and could turn and twist to deceive an opponent, but he didn't dribble with the ball.

Bert played for United in the 1901 and 1902 FA Cup finals and was capped against Wales in 1902. He was a cool, quiet and unassuming man but 'as sharp as a needle', and he represented United's players at the first meeting of the PFA (Professional Footballers Association) in 1907 and played a leading part in the development of the Player's Union. This, in part, led to him leaving the Lane. He had been injured and, when fit again, was chosen for the reserve team but refused to play, arguing with Arthur Neal, a United Football Committee member, that other senior players had been immediately selected for first-team duties after injury.

Lipsham was immediately suspended for seven days and quickly transferred to Fulham for £350. He later played for and then managed Millwall, coached West Norwood and managed Northfleet United, before emigrating to Canada in 1923. He died in Toronto in March 1932.

David Mercer
Outside right, 1920-28

	Appearances	Goals
League	223	22
FA Cup	18	0
FL Cup	-	-
Other	9	0
TOTAL	250	22

United were involved in a relegation struggle in December 1920 and spent heavily on two new players. The first was Fred Tunstall and the second was David Mercer, the Hull City outside right. United had no doubt recalled a wartime match played at Hull in 1919 when Mercer, then playing at inside right, had scored six goals. United had been late in arriving and played in borrowed boots; Hull led 6-1 when the game was abandoned in gathering darkness – although Mercer's goals counted for nothing, it was not a day easily forgotten.

Mercer was born in Skelmersdale in March 1893 and was transferred from the local team to Hull City in January 1914. He made his League debut in April of that year, embarking on a quite remarkable run of 218 consecutive appearances. United had secured his transfer for a near League record fee of £4,250, but Mercer seemed to lack confidence and only really began to play well when Tommy Sampy became his partner in March 1921. Mercer then began to justify the money that had been spent on him and played his part in United's narrow escape from relegation.

Stockily built, though never a vigorous player, Mercer was an extremely skilful outside right. He had played many games for Hull at inside right but only made occasional appearances in that position for United. References to 'twinkling feet' and the 'dancing master' give some impression of this quick and tricky player and a leading Sheffield journalist wrote of his 'model centres', which provided so many opportunities for United's other forwards.

He was a member of the FA tour of South Africa in 1920 and played for England against Ireland in October 1922 and, later that same season, against Belgium. He played for the Football League against the Scottish League in 1924 and was United's outside right in the 1925 FA Cup final.

David's brother, Arthur, was an inside right. He joined United in 1926 and the pair made over thirty appearances together before both were released in the summer of 1928. David had a period with Shirebrook in the Midland League and then played one final season in the League with Torquay United and later assisted Dartmouth United.

He settled in Torquay and one of his three sons also played for the local club. He died there in June 1950.

Ernest Milton
Left-back, 1917-27

	Appearances	Goals
League	203	3
FA Cup	17	1
FL Cup	-	-
Other	51	0
TOTAL	271	4

Ernest Milton was the United left-back in the 1925 Cup Final. He was born in Rotherham, in 1897, and was the younger brother of a Sunderland full-back who was killed during the First World War. Ernest was recommended to United while playing for Kilnhurst Town during that war and, after a game with the reserves, he was given a trial in a first-team match at the Lane against Huddersfield Town in January 1917. He acquitted himself well enough to be given further opportunities and was signed on amateur forms – professional terms were not possible during the war – at the end of that season.

Milton played in the first game of the following season but then was dropped or withdrew his services. He had apparently claimed that he had signed by 'misinterpretation'. He played a few games for Rotherham County, Birmingham and Barnsley but wrote to United in March 1919, offering his services and hoping there would be no 'ill-will' if he returned to the Lane.

Stocky, with thinning fair hair, he was a strong, bustling, resolute player, who tackled well and was difficult to beat. He was playing so well during the 1920/21 season that he was chosen for an FA eleven and the *Green 'Un* commented that, he 'should be in the England set up' but there were shortcomings in his play. He was two-footed and he could kick a ball at any angle, but he tended to 'balloon' the ball or clear it wildly and a columnist wrote in 1925 that Milton had 'hardly fulfilled early expectations'. It was during the 1924/25 season that United signed Len Birks and Milton, for a time, lost his first-team place. He came back, of course, and won an FA Cup medal.

Milton had a longstanding injury problem. That injury and the introduction of the new offside law (which put an emphasis on speed), ended his playing days. He set up a business and became a county standard bowls player. He died in Sheffield in 1984.

Tommy Morren
Centre half, 1895-1903

	Appearances	Goals
League	160	5
FA Cup	26	1
FL Cup	-	-
Other	4	0
TOTAL	190	6

The story of Tommy Morren's transfer to United in November 1895 is one of the great football legends. He was the United centre half in the great team that won the League Championship in 1898 and the FA Cup in the following year and he also played in the final of 1901. An English international, he was also an Amateur Cup winner with Middlesbrough.

Morren was born in the Monkwearmouth district of Sunderland in 1871. He joined Middlesbrough, who were then an amateur club, and played in their FA Cup-winning team of 1895. Phil Bache, who had captained the side, had become a professional with Reading and Morren, who had taken over the captaincy but was out of work, agreed to join him and become a professional.

Morren's train journey to Reading came via Sheffield, but United had received news of his plans from the Middlesbrough secretary. George Waller, the United trainer, who had played football and cricket in Middlesbrough and knew Morren, was sent down to the Midland station in Sheffield to persuade the player to have a trial with United. Waller was not a man for half measures; he grabbed Morren's bag from the rack in the carriage and made off in the direction of a waiting hansom cab with the poor player in tow, protesting that he was expected in Reading. He played that afternoon in a reserve game at the Lane and then returned to Middlesbrough, only agreeing to sign for United after the club agreed that he could continue with his job as a moulder.

Tommy was a member of the famous 'midget' United half-back line. He was 5ft 5in tall in height and was 'better in defence than in feeding his forwards' according to Ernest Needham. Morren was 'always in the thick of the action' and a player who fought to the last, and he talked incessantly on the field, trying to unsettle opponents. He was a victim of injuries and illness and missed some international and representative honours – indeed, in later years, he played with 'one leg and a swinger'. Eventually, he lost his place to Bernard Wilkinson.

Morren was released by United in 1904 and, after playing in a few friendly matches with the new Leeds City team, he gave up the game and kept a general store in the Sharrow district. He died in Sheffield in 1929.

Colin Morris
Outside right, 1982-88

	Appearances	Goals
League	240	67
FA Cup	17	5
FL Cup	20	7
Other	10	5
TOTAL	287	84

After Sheffield United had been relegated to the Fourth Division in 1980, Reg Brealey, the new chairman, appointed Ian Porterfield as manager and several new players were purchased in an attempt to make an immediate return to the Third. Results were reasonably successful, but at the beginning of February, Porterfield returned to the transfer market and signed Colin Morris from Blackpool for a bargain price of less than £100,000. The new man provided that little extra that sent the Blades on to win the championship.

Morris, a small, traditional right winger, had been born in August 1953 in Blyth in Northumberland. He had been on Burnley's books as a young player but had been released after a handful of games, moving to Southend United in 1977 and then, at the end of 1979, to Blackpool.

Morris was an instant success at the Lane. Blessed with two good feet, his darting runs, which combined both speed and trickery, provided Keith Edwards, in particular, with opportunities that were readily turned into goals and brought the Fourth Division championship to Bramall Lane. But there was a lot more to Morris – and indeed Edwards – than goals, for he provided skill and entertainment that spectators crave. Colin was also a good finisher himself and had an excellent record from the penalty spot, many of the awards coming after he himself had been brought down in the area by tormented defenders. He ended his days with United holding the club records for both penalties scored and missed.

Always consistent and a model professional, Colin was nearly thirty-five when he played his final match for United, scoring his side's only goal in the play-off semi-final against Bristol City. Dave Bassett was now the United manager and Colin joined Scarborough, where he later became the manager, before moving on to Boston United, Goole and Bridlington Town. Colin's son, Lee, became a United professional in 1997, but was transferred to Derby County in 1999.

Ernest 'Nudger' Needham
Left half, 1891-1910

	Appearances	Goals
League	464	49
FA Cup	49	12
FL Cup	-	-
Other	41	4
TOTAL	554	65

It would be extremely difficult, if not impossible, to argue a case against a proposal that Ernest Needham was Sheffield United's greatest-ever player and captain. An objective judgement can only be made based on the comments of his contemporaries and, even more so, by his record. Looking at it from these points of view, there really is no contest.

Needham was born in January 1873 in Newbold Moor, a district of Chesterfield, but his family moved when he was six to nearby Staveley. He played for a local boys' team and then, when he was sixteen, he joined the local Staveley club, a team of some standing in those days. Soon after his eighteenth birthday, having already played for the local association in Sheffield, he joined Sheffield United, making his first-team debut in a club fixture in September 1891 against the Royal Arsenal.

Needham was already spoken of as a fine player and yet lacked pace, weight and height – he was less than 5ft 6in tall (although the average height of men in those days was probably only around 5ft 8in). At first, United let him find his feet at outside right but he soon took over the left half spot in the United team (though in truth, he could and did play anywhere and frequently moved into the forward line if United were seeking a winning goal or equalizer and scored many a precious goal).

He was a clever player and tenacious, here, there, and everywhere on the field; indeed a criticism of his play was that he often tried to do too much. His main attributes were those of all great players: a superb sense of anticipation and ability to read the game, watching the ball like a hawk and playing apparently without a second's hesitation over his next move. He tackled keenly but was never cautioned, he dribbled superbly and finished well and his play was described as making him a faultless 'football machine'.

The mantle of greatness lay well on the shoulders of Ernest Needham. Referred to frequently by his contemporaries as the 'Prince of half-backs', Needham was the United captain when the club won the Football League Championship in 1898 and two of United's four FA Cup triumphs, United capturing the trophy in 1899 and 1902 and reaching the final in 1901. For a period of over eight years, Needham was also an automatic selection (when fit) for England, winning 16 caps (seven of them against Scotland) – which was a massive number in those days – and was one of the first professional players to captain England. It was a remarkable history of achievement and it is worth bearing in mind that United were

Needham leads United onto the field. The other players are Captain Hedley, Morren, Beer and Foulke.

playing in the Northern League when Needham first played for them in 1891, but within eight years the club was at the very pinnacle of British football, having won the League Championship and beaten Glasgow Celtic, the Scottish champions, in a challenge match.

'Nudger' was a fine captain and saved United on many an occasion, particularly in cup-ties when all seemed lost. He would change the tactics and formation of the team – not an idea that current managers will comprehend – and had the ability to raise the morale and efforts of the United players while, at the same time, fomenting doubts and a sense of impending failure in the minds of the opposition. Contemporaries regarded Needham as one of the greatest leaders, yet it is interesting that he once wrote that the position of captain as being 'a proud one' but not always 'a pleasant position'.

His final first-team appearance was in 1910, when he was thirty-seven, but he coached the reserves for a short time and acted as a scout. Needham also played cricket for eleven seasons for Derbyshire and topped the batting averages in 1908. He died in March 1936, but distant years cannot deny the record of a truly great footballer who was described by a fellow international as – taking all aspects of the game into consideration – the 'greatest player, association football has ever seen'.

Albert Nightingale
Centre forward/inside right, 1941-48

	Appearances	Goals
League	62	15
FA Cup	10	2
FL Cup	-	-
Other	153	71
TOTAL	225	88

Some of the players of yesteryear might have had difficulties coming to terms with contemporary patterns of play, but the crowded penalty areas of the modern era would have been meat and drink to Albert Nightingale, who could weave his way through a defence with the ball seemingly glued to his feet. Albert wasn't a stylish player, but he was extremely difficult to stop.

Nightingale was born in Thrybergh in November 1923 and had brothers who were also footballers: Ken and Sam had played for Rotherham United and Lawrence was a trainer there and later at the Lane. Albert was a miner during the Second World War and was playing for Thurcroft Colliery when he came to United's attention.

His first game for United was on Easter Monday 1941 at Hillsborough and he had another trial in September with the reserves at Denaby. In November, he played centre forward at Rotherham and held his place in the team. He was small for a striker but he was aggressive, worked hard and was difficult to knock off the ball. For the next four seasons, he averaged a goal in every other game playing centre forward or at inside right. His first hat-trick came in 1943 and he scored four goals against Chesterfield in January 1944. He was top scorer that season and again in 1945/46 when United won the Football League North championship.

He played at inside right that season and, although he had another spell at centre forward when First Division football resumed, he was now regarded as an inside forward. He continued to work as a miner, however, because of Britain's post-war economic problems.

He asked for a transfer early in 1948, and moved to Huddersfield Town in an exchange deal, United taking two players (Graham Bailey and George Hutchinson) and £10,000. He moved on to Blackburn Rovers in October 1951 (£12,000) and finally, in October 1952, to Leeds United (£10,000). His happiest season turned out to be his last, as Leeds, with Nightingale, Harold Brook – his former partner at the Lane – and John Charles as their forward trio, swept into the First Division. For Albert, tragedy struck in the first game of the new season when he was injured (Leeds were leading 5-0 at the time) and never played again.

His style of play changed over the years. During the war, he had played seemingly with 'only one object; to try and bore his way through a defence single-handed'. He was tenacious, 'hard as nails and difficult to charge off the ball' with a fine 'body swerve and strong ball control' and he would emerge from a ruck of players with the ball, when it seemed impossible. Later, he became a more typical inside forward but he was always strong and direct, and terrier-like in his determination to win.

Roger Nilsen
Left-back/Central defender, 1993-99

	Appearances	Goals
League	166	0
FA Cup	11	0
FL Cup	10	0
Other	3	0
TOTAL	190	0

How do you explain it? How can an international footballer of quality; admittedly a defender, fail to score a single goal from open play for the Blades when he had a kick like a mule and was a good header of the ball?

Roger Nilsen, a fair-haired Norwegian defender from Tromso, was born in August 1969. He was signed by Dave Bassett in November 1993 from the Viking club in Stavanger for an initial fee of £400,000, which ultimately rose to £650,000. Roger had 16 full international caps when he joined United and, apart from an eight-month loan spell with Cologne in Germany, had played all his football in Norway.

Nilsen made his Premier League debut at Norwich in a team which included fellow countryman, Jostein Flo, but it was a season which ended in relegation in the cruel circumstances of possible match-fixing. The summer held further disappointment, for although Nilsen was a member of the Norwegian World Cup party that headed off to the United States, he was fated, unlike Flo, never to play.

The best moments of his time at the Lane were probably the quarter-final FA Cup tie against Coventry City when he netted one of the vital shoot-out penalties – this was the only goal of his United career – and the semi-final at Old Trafford against Newcastle United, but he missed many games because of injury and they included the play-off games against Sunderland at the end of that same season.

Before he came to Sheffield, Nilsen had played in the left centre of the defence and that was the position he always preferred but, initially, Bassett used him at left-back and Roger played well in both positions. He was a strong player, tackled firmly and was good in the air. His kicking was clean, powerful and crisp and Unitedites eagerly waited for his first goal, knowing that he had a good record for a defender in his homeland. The shots rained in, but that goal never came. It also has to be noted that Roger – very occasionally and quite out of character considering his general high standards – had some amazing lapses, usually leaving the United goalkeeper totally exposed. If United got away with it, they were quite amusing.

Roger's contract ended in 1999 and he was aware, following talks with manager Steve Bruce, that it would not be extended. Surprisingly, however, he spent his last few weeks of English football making three appearances with Tottenham Hotspur, who signed him in March 1999 on a free transfer as emergency cover.

Derek 'Doc' Pace
Centre forward, 1957-64

	Appearances	Goals
League	253	140
FA Cup	31	18
FL Cup	10	5
Other	8	12
TOTAL	302	175

A player respected by friend and foe alike, 'Doc' Pace was one of United's most successful and popular centre forwards. He wasn't a big man, but had that sharpness, awareness, determination and courage that all great strikers require. He timed his runs to perfection and his finishing, particularly with his head, was both fearless and superb.

Pace came from Essington, a village near Wolverhampton, and played his early football for Bloxwich Strollers before signing, when he was seventeen, for Aston Villa. His National Service was spent in the Royal Army Medical Corps and earned him the nickname 'Doc', but he was unable to establish a regular first-team place at Villa Park and was unlucky when Villa won the FA Cup in 1957 to be chosen only as the twelfth man.

He was energetic, tenacious and willing to take knocks.. He always seemed to play well against United and scored a hat-trick against them in April 1956 as the Blades dropped into the Second Division. Joe Mercer, United's manager, had earlier tried to sign Pace and finally succeeded in December 1957, Derek making his debut on Boxing Day. 'Doc' arrived at the Lane that day and heard a disgruntled supporter say 'Another little 'un', but he scored after eight minutes and the goals continued to flow from this prolific scoring player.

For seven successive seasons, 'Doc' was the Blades' leading scorer, showing a fearless determination to reach the ball in the penalty area. He scored four goals on one occasions and six hat-tricks, including a memorable one at Villa Park, and was always at his best against the Owls. He had an excellent scoring record in the FA Cup (and indeed United put in some fine performances in that competition during his time at the Lane). He surprisingly lost his scoring touch when United reached the semi-final in 1961, but his 26 goals in the League helped secure promotion.

Derek's soccer career ended rather quickly. He played in the first three games of the 1964/65 season, but then had a stomach operation and was transferred to Notts County and brought his League career to a close with a few games at Walsall. Derek worked as a representative and coached a Walsall amateur club, but died in 1981 at the age of fifty-seven, following a heart attack.

Harold Pantling
Wing half, 1915-25

	Appearances	Goals
League	224	1
FA Cup	20	0
FL Cup	-	-
Other	124	1
TOTAL	368	2

There is a certain fascination about the 'hard men' of football, and it could be said that Harold Pantling was one of that breed. In his defence, many of his misdemeanours were due to his seeking retribution for fouls committed on other United players and one colleague denied that he was a 'hard man', explaining that it was largely bluff – his reputation being sufficient to frighten many opponents. There were other qualities to his game, however, and he well deserved the England cap that he was awarded in 1923.

Born in Leighton Buzzard in May 1891, Pantling joined Watford in 1908 as an amateur and signed as a professional in the close season of 1911. Playing mainly at right-back or at right half, Pantling secured a regular place in the Watford team in April 1913 and he joined United a year later along with Ashbridge, an inside forward, the Blades paying £850 for the pair. Pantling made his first-team debut in February 1915, during the season in which United defeated Chelsea in the FA Cup final.

Pantling began to claim a regular first-team place during the wartime 1915/16 season and proved his versatility by turning out in both full-back and half-back positions. It wasn't long before opponents knew that he wasn't a player to trifle with. He was sent off twice during the 1917/18 season and dismissed again in 1921 – although press reports indicate that the referee's decision was severe.

Harold's play wasn't stylish. His tackling was resolute, but also clever and shrewd, and his heading was good. Sound, dependable, hardworking and consistent are the words that best describe the man who became a fixture in the United side at right half-back in the early years of the 1920s and who became a member of the PFA's management committee. He had also proved, while he was with Watford, to be a capable stand-in goalkeeper and in August 1923 he had the distinction, having taken Gough's place in goal, of saving a penalty kick with his first touch of the ball in the first League match played on the new Manchester City ground at Maine Road.

In the autumn of 1924, United, with Pantling now thirty-three years of age, paid a large fee for Bruce Longworth, the Bolton Wanderers wing half, and Pantling's first-team days looked to be over. The new man was soon injured, however, and Pantling was recalled to the first team and went on to play in the successful 1925 Cup Final side. A year later he was released, joined Rotherham United and became a licensee, later having a short spell with Heanor Town. He died in Sheffield in December 1952.

Jack Pickering
Inside forward, 1927-48

	Appearances	Goals
League	344	102
FA Cup	23	9
FL Cup	-	-
Other	194	80
TOTAL	561	191

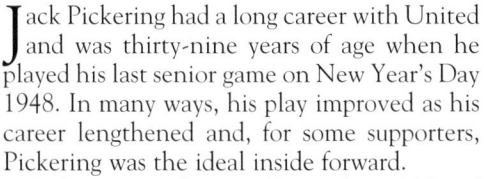

Jack Pickering had a long career with United and was thirty-nine years of age when he played his last senior game on New Year's Day 1948. In many ways, his play improved as his career lengthened and, for some supporters, Pickering was the ideal inside forward.

Pickering was born in December 1908 and came from the High Green area to the north east of Sheffield. He was educated at Barnsley Grammar School and played for Mortomley St Saviours. United gave him a trial with the reserves in April 1925 when he was sixteen and he made his first-team debut in 1927.

Because of his intelligence and style of play, Pickering was groomed as the successor to Billy Gillespie, the United inside left and captain. The idea seemed sensible enough, but in practice it was many years before it really came to fruition. Jack wanted to be a part-time player and told United in 1929 that he had found a suitable office job. United were not well pleased when they discovered that the 'office' belonged to a turf accountant and put a stop to it. Pickering went on to train successfully as a chartered accountant.

Pickering was tall and slim, with a long stride. He could finish with a powerful and accurate shot but his temperament was somewhat of a problem and he tended to play well 'only in flashes'. He was capped by England against Scotland in 1933, but other major honours never followed and a few months after winning his international cap, United, not for the first time, relegated him to the reserve team – only to discover that he had scored all six goals against Preston North End.

Pickering was a player who 'let the ball do the work' and rarely dribbled, feeling that he had 'done something wrong if he had to beat a player'. Jack made football seem such a simple game. He found space, called for the ball, sent out measured passes and finished with fierce but accurate shots.

Although United were relegated in 1934, Jack Pickering's thoughtful, constructive play made him a vital player in the 1936 team that were FA Cup finalists and narrowly missed out on promotion and he was a leading figure in the promotion team of 1939. He captained United through most of the war years and had a vital role in the development of young players such as Fred Furniss, Harry Latham, Harold Brook, Albert Nightingale and Alec Forbes.

He left Sheffield in 1948 and managed and coached Poole Town. Later he became a Bournemouth hotelier and died in that town in May 1977.

Fred Priest
Left winger/inside forward, 1896-1905

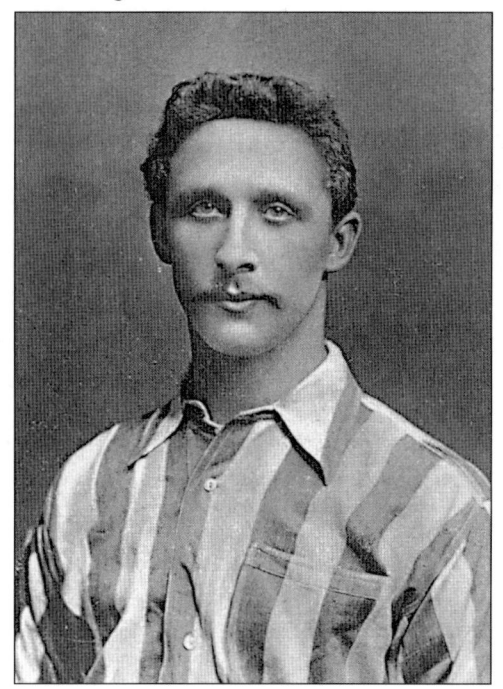

	Appearances	Goals
League	209	68
FA Cup	37	18
FL Cup	-	-
Other	2	0
TOTAL	248	86

Fred Priest was not a player who frequently attracted headlines, but the part he played in the great United team that came together in the closing years of the reign of Queen Victoria should not be underestimated. In particular, he will be remembered as a player who seldom failed on the big occasion and scored vital goals.

Alfred Ernest Priest was born at South Bank, near Middlesbrough, in July 1875. He played for the local side and was just one of the many players from that part of England who came to the Lane in the mid and late 1890s. His first appearance in our colours was in April 1896 at Newcastle in a friendly match – although match reports mention his appearance as a 'trial', in reality he had been a registered United player since February.

Playing at outside left, Fred scored on his League debut and played a full part when United won the League Championship in 1898 and the FA Cup at the end of the following season. He was capped against Ireland in 1900. The signing of Bert Lipsham in 1900 and injuries cost Priest his place in the side but he returned as Lipsham's partner to score vital goals in the FA Cup campaign of 1901, when United were losing finalists, and in 1902 when Southampton were defeated in the final.

Priest's last season was essentially that of 1904/05, when he played for a time at left-back, before he moved to Middlesbrough in August 1906 on a free transfer to act as their trainer with permission to play occasionally. In 1908, he joined Hartlepool as a player-manager and remained with the club until 1915.

Priest was a popular player. He was fair-haired and blessed with a sunny temperament, but he was also determined, tenacious and difficult to knock off the ball. He had a fair turn of speed with the ability to gather a pass on the run and put across a fine centre. It was said that he had 'a heart like a lion,' and 'no defence was too strong for him'.

When he finished playing, he kept the Market Hotel in Hartlepool and died there in reduced circumstances in May 1922. United played a benefit game for his widow and family, with Alf Common, his old colleague, as the referee.

Gil Reece
Outside left, 1965-72

	Appearances	Goals
League	211	59
FA Cup	8	1
FL Cup	12	2
Other	10	5
TOTAL	241	67

There wasn't much to Gilbert Ivor Reece (5ft 7in tall and less than 10 st in weight), but he was a determined character and extremely tough. Born in Cardiff in July 1942, he was a Welsh schoolboy international outside left and also a useful boxer. He failed to make the grade with Cardiff City, but signed for Newport County as a part-timer after playing with Pembroke Borough. He made his League debut for Newport County in October 1963 in a Fourth Division match against Workington and, after 32 appearances during which he scored 9 goals, he was transferred to United.

The signing, which took place in April 1965, was a rare excursion into the transfer market by John Harris, the United manager, but it was surely one he never regretted, although 'Gil' did provide him with a few problems. United paid £10,000 for his services and he made his debut for the Blades in May 1965 in a local County Cup final game at Doncaster, scoring two goals.

There was never any doubt at Bramall Lane that Reece would be successful and he was awarded the first of his 29 Welsh caps in October 1965. He was fast and clever, a good finisher and a fine header of the ball, but he also tackled hard and he had the will to succeed.

He played an important role in the promotion season of 1970/71, but then lost his place to Stewart Scullion. Reece was a proud man with a stubborn streak who hated being dropped or given a place on the substitutes' bench, and this brought problems for the player and his managers. He was suspended by United on one occasion and also walked out on the Welsh team in 1970, resenting the position, as it seemed to him, of being a permanent non-playing substitute. He was transferred to Cardiff City in 1972 and took part in their promotion campaign of 1975/76, but was then given a free transfer and returned to playing as a part-timer.

The recent news that he has had to have part of a leg amputated was received with great sadness by all those United supporters who remember his determined displays.

Brian Richardson
Right half-back, 1955-65

	Appearances	Goals
League	291	9
FA Cup	28	0
FL Cup	10	0
Other	7	0
TOTAL	336	9

Brian Richardson wasn't a stylish player, but he played a vital part in the famous Sheffield United defence that first played together in September 1957 and made their final appearance in August 1963. (It would be difficult for any United supporter of those days to remember any one of the six players without thinking of the complete defence as a whole.)

A report in the Sheffield *Star & Green 'Un* described Brian, when he was fifteen, as a 'good strong tackling player, making up for his lack of constructive ability by determination and tirelessness.' The writer would have no reason to change his opinions as the years went by. Richardson was the quintessential midfield player, but his primary role was defensive and he was rarely seen in the opposition penalty area. His strengths were close marking, razor-sharp tackling and covering; he was ever watchful to nip attacks in the bud or to force opponents into less dangerous positions and he was good in the air.

He was born in Sheffield in October 1934 and had played for Sheffield Boys at both cricket and football, but it was hard work and determination rather than natural talent that made him a successful First Division player. He spent three years as an amateur on United's books before becoming a professional and it wasn't until 1955, when he was twenty years old, that he made his first-team debut on a close-season tour in Germany. He made his League debut at Luton late in that same year, playing, as he frequently did in those days, at centre half.

Joe Mercer, the United manager, gave Brian the chance to establish a regular place in the first team in September 1957, taking over the right half position from Tommy Hoyland, and Richardson's success owed much to the coaching and encouragement he received from the former England wing half. Richardson's inclusion in the team completed the famous six-man defence which would take the Blades to the semi-final stage of the 1961 FA Cup and see the club return to the First Division.

A colleague summed up Brian's importance to that fine team. He was 'all heart and guts and strength' and 'greatly under-rated by his opponents'. He lost his first-team place in 1965 to David Munks and was sold in January 1966 to Swindon Town for £3,000, before moving at the end of that season to play for Rochdale.

Walter Rickett
Winger, 1940-47

	Appearances	Goals
League	57	16
FA Cup	9	0
FL Cup	-	-
Other	210	58
TOTAL	276	74

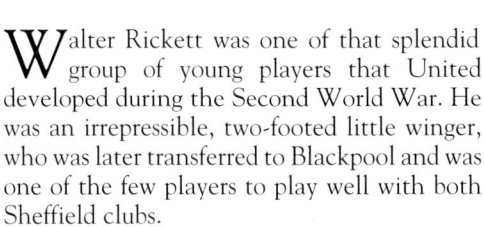

Walter Rickett was one of that splendid group of young players that United developed during the Second World War. He was an irrepressible, two-footed little winger, who was later transferred to Blackpool and was one of the few players to play well with both Sheffield clubs.

He was born in Sheffield in March 1917 and played for the Aqueduct club. Although he was only 5ft 6in in height, he came to United as a centre forward, but the club used him as a winger, playing him in the 'A' team towards the end of the last peacetime season. Walter's first-team debut was at Rochdale in January 1940 and United failed to score, but he did score on his third outing with the first team, his first kick deceiving Morton, the Owls' goalkeeper.

Rickett had a reserved occupation, so he was able to play for United throughout the war. He usually played at outside left but also appeared on the other wing. He was a lively character, dangerous when cutting in and a regular goal-scorer, but he was an instinctive player – the *Sheffield Telegraph* commenting, late in 1944, that he 'does not seem to know what to do with the ball when in possession'. He was seen at his best in the 1945/46 season, when United won the League North championship and in the first post-war season; indeed, it was his goal in the last game that prevented Stoke City winning the championship.

There was 'no player more wholehearted and enthusiastic' than Walter. He was 'without an atom of fear in his make-up' and 'as tough as the steel manufactured in his native city'. He also seemed to shrug off injuries; Duggie Livingstone, the trainer, once spotted Walter limping along the far wing and commented, 'Walter has broken his leg'. He was 'a bundle of energy' and as 'lively as a cricket' but he had his limitations. Schemes worked out in training were forgotten once the whistle blew. He 'needed the ball in front of him. He was no good if he had to stop and think' for he was 'not sure what to do with the ball'.

He was exchanged for George Farrow of Blackpool in January 1948, which was a total disaster for United. Rickett played splendidly in the 1948 Cup Final against Manchester United but returned to Sheffield in October 1949, joining Wednesday for £6,000. In his stay with the Owls, they were promoted, relegated and Second Division championship winners, with Walter being awarded an England 'B' cap.

He also played for Rotherham United, Halifax Town, Ballymena United and Dundalk. He was a player-manager with Ards and then manager of Sittingbourne, Ramsgate and Gravesend, and assistant manager with the Orient. He died in July 1991 in Kettering Hospital.

Alf Ringstead
Outside right, 1950-59

	Appearances	Goals
League	247	101
FA Cup	13	4
FL Cup	-	-
Other	11	4
TOTAL	271	109

Although he was brought up in England, Alf Ringstead had never seen a Football League game until he played in one. He was twenty-three when he made his United debut and his impact was remarkable, for he scored 56 goals in his first 106 League games – an outstanding scoring rate for a wing forward. In later years, he was but a shadow of the player he had been but this does not tarnish memories of a great player at his best.

Alfred Ringstead was born in Dublin on 14 October 1927. He was the son of a well-known jockey, but Alf was too stocky to follow in his father's footsteps. His mother was Irish but the family moved to England when he was a two years old and settled in Ellesmere Port. Alf's talents as a footballer led him to join Everton when he was fourteen, but the young player never felt part of the club, feeling that he received neither advice or encouragement, and he rejected a trial with Bolton Wanderers, feeling that he would be happier playing in local football with Ellesmere Port.

Ringstead became an upholsterer and, later, a coach fitter. He served in the Army in India and took a step up the football ladder when he joined Northwich Victoria, a Cheshire League side, for £200 in 1950. He came to United's notice when he had scored eleven goals after just a handful of games. United watched him in a game at Buxton in November 1950 and he was signed a few days later. Alf was twenty-three and the fee was £2,500.

After two Central League games, Ringstead made his League debut against Coventry City at the Lane and was an immediate success, scoring one goal with a flying header, winning a penalty kick (which Harold Brook sent high over the bar) and playing with such confidence and skill that it was obvious that he would have a fine future in the game. Some players take time to adjust, but Ringstead moved from the Cheshire League to become an instant star in the Second Division, scoring in his first three games and winning the first of his 20 Irish caps at the end of that season.

His ability and confidence was remarkable for an 'unknown' newcomer to League football and he established a League record (to the best knowledge of this author) for a wing forward by scoring 100 goals in his first 208 games. He was fortunate of course, in that he was at his best when United had other excellent players and outstanding forwards. Unitedites who can look back to the entertaining team of the early 1950s will remember Alf cutting in and latching onto balls threaded through the defence by Brook or Hagan, or popping up in the six-yard box to meet a centre from Hawksworth or a knock-down from Browning.

He was United's leading scorer in 1951/52 and again in the Second Division championship season of 1952/53. For four or five years, Alf was one of the most dangerous wingers in

A typical action shot of Alf.

the business. He was fast and direct and able to shoot with power and accuracy with both feet, but surprisingly for such a good striker of the ball, he failed to score with the three penalties he took – though all required fine saves by the opposing 'keeper. Ringstead was also a superb header of the ball, confident in diving full-length, if necessary, to meet a low centre. These strengths would have been enough to make him potentially a top-class player, but the factors that made him truly outstanding were his sense of anticipation that took him into goal-scoring positions, and the ability to lose his marker. 'It has always been my policy', he said, 'to keep the opposing full-back looking for me and that's why I cut in so often'.

Injuries eventually took their toll, and the consequent loss of speed stole the edge from his game. Alf was never as happy playing for Joe Mercer as he had been with Reg Freeman, and he was a pale imitation of the player of the early 1950s that few defenders could tame. He was, however, still able to achieve an unusual hat-trick of headers in 1958 against Scunthorpe United before he lost his place to Kevin Lewis.

Ringstead was transferred to Mansfield Town in 1959 for £2,850 and later played for Frickley Colliery, Buxton and Macclesfield. He died in Sheffield in January 2000.

Bill Russell
Inside forward, 1957-63

	Appearances	Goals
League	144	55
FA Cup	23	15
FL Cup	4	0
Other	3	3
TOTAL	174	73

Bill Russell was still an amateur when he first played for United. He was the last such player to appear for the first team and also the last amateur international and major part-time footballer to play for the Blades.

Bill was born in Hounslow (Middlesex) in July 1935. His father had been a professional with Chelsea and Hearts and was the former manager of Rhyl, where Bill was playing, when Joe Mercer, the United manager, signed him in August 1957. Russell, who was training to be a teacher, had played and scored for Bishop Auckland in the Amateur Cup final that year and was still an amateur when he made his debut for United in a reserve match at Bolton. He scored twice and was given his first-team debut at the Valley, along with Gerry Summers, and scored again.

In an arrangement that allowed Rhyl to capitalize on their player and Russell to win 4 amateur caps, he delayed becoming a professional with Rhyl until mid-November and almost immediately signed professional forms for United, Rhyl receiving £1,000 and the total receipts from two games that were played between the two clubs plus an additional later payment. He remained a part-time player, working first as a secondary school teacher and then as head of languages at a Further Education College in Altrincham.

He was fast and direct with good ball control, working assiduously in midfield and breaking rapidly – with the ability to move the ball accurately and at speed to his colleagues and always with an eye for goal. His shooting was sharp, crisp and accurate and his goal-scoring record, particularly in the FA Cup, was excellent.

He missed much of the 1959/60 season, breaking his leg at Bristol while playing at outside right. This was a problem area for United and he retained that position when the 1960/61 promotion season began, but a run of three defeats led Harris, the manager, to restore Bill to inside right. He had a splendid run, scoring eleven goals in ten games and in every round of the FA Cup up to the semi-final. These strikes included the only goal at Everton and a sixth round hat-trick in the first eighteen minutes at Newcastle.

In the following season, Bill scored in the fourth and fifth rounds of the FA Cup, but a crippling first-minute injury to Summers (in those pre-substitute days) halted any hopes of another semi-final and it was a sad but fitting close to his career at the Lane that his last appearance in United colours should be in a fifth round FA Cup tie in 1963.

He was transferred in March 1963 to Bolton Wanderers (£20,000) and later played for Rochdale, Scarborough and Chorley.

Geoff Salmons
Midfielder, 1966-74 and 1977

	Appearances	Goals
League	185	8
FA Cup	7	1
FL Cup	12	0
Other	15	1
TOTAL	219	10

Geoff Salmons, a long-striding, fast and strong left-sided player, established a permanent place in the United team when he played his part in the vital last five games of the successful push for promotion in 1971. He was sold to Stoke City during the close season of 1974 to relieve some of United's pressing financial problems, though he returned to the Lane on loan for five games in 1977.

Geoff was one of several Don & Dearne schoolboys who came to the Lane during the 1960s. He was born in Mexborough in January 1948 and became a United professional when he was eighteen. He played at first on the left wing, but moved inside and then into midfield – although his pace and stamina meant that he could cover a great deal of ground during any one game and surging runs from deep were always a feature of his play. His right foot was always weak, but his hard work was appreciated and his popularity with supporters was well deserved.

United's manager, Ken Furphy, said that his transfer to Stoke (for a sum of between £165,000 and 180,000) was 'purely for financial reasons' and also recognized that Salmons, who had a powerful left foot, should have scored more goals. Tony Waddington, the Stoke manager, was reported as saying that Salmons 'was a player who always gave us a lot of trouble'. Geoff had three seasons at the Victoria Ground and then had five games on loan with United in the autumn of 1977, but it was a time of turmoil at the Lane and Jimmy Sirrel, the manager, was sacked soon after.

Stoke transferred Salmons to Leicester and Geoff was one of the few satisfactory players in a disappointing City side, who ultimately were relegated. His next move, in August 1978, proved to be a happier one, Chesterfield paying a club record fee of £35,000 to bring him to Saltergate. He played well with Chesterfield and was deservedly popular with the fans, scoring one of the goals when Chesterfield completed a double over United at the Lane in 1980, and he was a member of the Anglo-Scottish Cup-winning team in the following season. Injuries hastened the end of his playing career but Geoff, now living in his native South Yorkshire, has continued to please the customers as a successful licensee and restaurant owner.

Tommy Sampy
Inside right/right half, 1921-34

	Appearances	Goals
League	340	27
FA Cup	31	5
FL Cup	-	-
Other	10	1
TOTAL	381	33

Tommy Sampy had a long and by no means unsuccessful soccer career, but it didn't provide the personal satisfaction that it should have done and there were occasions when he felt that his time in football had been wasted. A major reason, though probably not the only one, was Sampy's omission from the 1925 FA Cup final team.

Tommy was born in Backworth, Northumberland, in March 1899. He was an engineer and played for Choppington, South Shields, and Chopwell Colliery Institute in County Durham before signing for United in November 1920; he was joined, at the end of that season, by his brother Bill, who was a full-back. Tommy was a hardworking, terrier-like, clever inside forward and made his first-team debut in February of the same season. He grabbed a goal on his debut, but he wasn't a natural scorer.

The 1925 Cup Final must have been a defining moment in Sampy's life. The only position in doubt was that of inside right. It lay between Sampy – who had played in the two previous rounds – and Tommy Boyle. Sampy would later say, in private, that he and the other players hadn't played 'flat out' in the League matches leading up to the Cup Final, fearing injury. There was no lack of threats from opponents to put them out of the big game and, no doubt, the United players felt it was sensible to save themselves for Wembley. The only exception had been Boyle who, when given a first-team opportunity, had played really hard and with enthusiasm, no doubt encouraged by his father, an FA Cup winner with United in 1902. Sampy learned half an hour before the Cup Final kick-off that Boyle would play. Later, he was quoted as saying that the selection was correct and that he would have chosen Boyle.

Tommy moved to right half in the autumn of 1925 and, apart from the 1926/27 season when he was injured, played regularly until 1931, taking the captaincy from Billy Gillespie during the 1930/31 season. Sampy was an intelligent man and a popular player, but when the following season began, he lost his first-team place to Harry Gooney.

In 1934, after fourteen seasons at the Lane, he joined Barnsley – where he acted in the main as a coach – and then, a year later, Sheffield Wednesday. He was one of the early FA coaches working in South Yorkshire, but then returned to engineering as a production manager. He died in Sheffield in 1978.

Graham Shaw
Left-back, 1952-67

	Appearances	Goals
League	439	14
FA Cup	37	0
FL Cup	9	1
Other	13	0
TOTAL	498	15

Graham was a calm and stylish international left full-back who will always be remembered for his first-team debut as a seventeen-year-old in a Sheffield derby game at Hillsborough (in front of the record post-war gate of over 65,000). Shaw was awarded 5 full England caps and was a regular member of the United Championship side of 1952/53. He played in the famous defence that came together under Joe Mercer and then, under John Harris, won promotion and reached the semi-final of the FA Cup in 1961.

Graham Shaw was born in Sheffield on 9 July 1934 and was educated at the Pye Bank and Southey Green Schools. He played as a goalkeeper and then at centre half, but was moved to left-back by Sheffield Boys. He also played for Yorkshire Boys and was an all-round athlete, excelling at cricket and boxing – in which he was an ABA junior champion. Graham was invited by Duggie Livingstone, the United trainer and coach, to train at Bramall Lane and to play for the Sheffield United nursery club, Oaks Fold. He also played for United's reserve team and signed for the Blades on his seventeenth birthday, agreeing to concentrate on football and drop boxing.

His first-team debut was remarkable. United had begun the 1951/52 season in storming fashion and their victories had included one of 7-3 against Sheffield Wednesday. This was also Derek Dooley's record-breaking season for the Owls and their supporters waited with feverish anticipation for United's comeuppance in the return fixture, particularly as the United defence had begun to leak goals at a rather alarming rate.

United's full-backs that season were Fred Furniss and Albert Cox, but Cox was thirty-four and began to show signs that his first-team days were coming to an end. His deputy, Maurice McLafferty, wasn't good enough and in any case, on the morning of the return match with the Owls, he failed a fitness test. Graham had played just six or seven games for the reserves when he was given his first-team opportunity. Has any other British player made his debut in a local derby at the age of seventeen before a crowd of over 65,000? Teddy Davison, the United manager, had no qualms in choosing him for the fixture and the young player more than held his own as United ran out 3-1 winners.

Reg Freeman, who replaced Davison as the United manager, reintroduced Graham into the United team in September 1952 and he was a regular member of the Second Division championship side of that season. He missed much of the 1955/56 relegation season under Joe Mercer, because he was serving in the

Graham with Cec Coldwell.

Royal Signals. In the following season, Mercer played him at right-back, then at outside right, and tried to sell him to Stoke City. Graham refused to go and was reinstated in his usual position; Mercer later apologized for his treatment of the player.

It was Mercer who created and coached the great longstanding United defence, which included Graham – along with Alan Hodgkinson, Cec Coldwell, Brian Richardson, Joe Shaw (who was not related) and Gerry Summers. Under Harris, the 1960/61 team won promotion back to the First Division and reached the semi-final stage of the FA Cup when, unusually for Graham, he missed a penalty kick.

Graham was awarded 5 England under-23 caps and his first full cap was against Russia in 1958. He won 5 in all and also appeared for the Football League. In appearance, Graham was immaculate; his football was the perfect match, always displaying rare composure, authority and style. This was his hallmark and it was never lost. His tackling was perfectly timed and was both swift and accurate. His distribution, both long and short, was made with care and he covered well and was always available to receive a pass from a colleague. He played at left-back, although he preferred to use his more natural right foot.

He was the elder brother of Bernard Shaw and they made three appearances together in March 1965. His final League appearance in United colours came as an inside right in October 1966, against West Bromwich Albion, with his benefit match against the Wednesday following in April.

He was transferred in September 1967 to Doncaster Rovers and then had a year as the player-manager of Scarborough, but injuries led to him leaving by 'mutual consent'. He ran a snack bar in the Sheffield Castle Market and was the licensee of the Sportsman Inn. Graham was the chairman of the Future Blades Fund and also served as captain and president of the Dore & Totley Golf Club. He died in Sheffield in May 1998.

Joe Shaw
Wing-half/centre half, 1945-66

	Appearances	Goals
League	632	7
FA Cup	51	0
FL Cup	7	0
Other	24	1
TOTAL	714	8

Joe Shaw was one of United's greatest ever players and a joy to watch in the centre of the defence, yet few who watched Joe in his early years would have expressed the view that he would become a superb player. He holds the record for the highest number of League appearances by a Sheffield United player and was one of the youngest ever to turn out for the Blades.

He was born in Murton (County Durham) in June 1928, but his family moved to South Yorkshire when he was a boy. Joe was an inside forward playing for Upton Colliery when he came to United's attention. The war in Europe was drawing to a close and the United manager of the time was looking to the future. Shaw's debut as a sixteen-year-old was unusual, for Joe had never trained with United and the first intimation that he had that United were interested in him was a postcard informing him that 'You are selected to play v. Huddersfield Town at Bramall Lane Ground, on Easter Monday next, 2 April 1945. Report at Dressing Room at 2.15 p.m.'

His debut was uneventful, the *Sheffield Telegraph* report failing to give him a mention and, after one further outing with the first team, the young man spent the next three years in the Central League side. Playing as an inside forward, Joe was energetic and full of enthusiasm but he wasn't equipped with searing pace, clinical finishing ability, superb passing or creative skills. Joe developed slowly, however, and it was not until August 1948 that he made his League debut against Liverpool.

Joe had played at wing half as early as May 1947 but it was not until the autumn of 1948 that he began to play there regularly. The move to wing half led to a huge improvement in Shaw's prospects as a footballer and in February 1949 his swift and decisive tackling and enthusiastic all-round play won him a permanent place at left half. Shaw never looked back and he was a member of the 1952/53 Second Division championship team. He took over the captain's role in 1954, and that was also the year when he began to play regularly at centre half.

Joe Shaw was unlucky not to be awarded a full England cap. He was chosen in 1955 as the official reserve for England against Scotland – there was no squad of players in those days – but when wing half Len Phillips dropped out, Ken Armstrong was chosen ahead of Shaw. The reason, it was assumed, was that Shaw, that season, was playing at centre half.

There is little doubt that number five was his best position. He had played centre half for the reserve team as early as 1949 and, for the first team in 1950 and in those pre-substitute days, if the number five was injured during the game, Joe would take over the centre spot. As he stood just 5ft 8in tall, he wasn't a natural for the position, but he had begun to show a

February 1965. Joe, Brian Richardson, Alan Woodward and Reg Matthewson take the field at Bramall Lane.

rare ability to read the game, anticipating the opposition's moves.

It was Reg Freeman, one of United's finest managers, who gave Shaw the centre half berth (after first trying Cec Coldwell in the number five shirt) and made him captain. Joe had still quite a bit to learn, particularly when facing some of the big heavyweight centre forwards of the day and Joe Mercer, who succeeded Freeman as our manager, initially preferred a big number five – eventually restoring Joe to the centre and building the great defence that older Unitedites remember with pride.

Alan Hodgkinson, Cec Coldwell, Graham Shaw (who was not related to Joe), Brian Richardson and Gerry Summers first played together on 7 September 1957, and they were fortunate in that they suffered very few injuries. They formed the defence in the promotion team of 1961, which also reached the FA Cup semi-final and fought so well in many other cup campaigns, and it was not until the 31 August 1963 that they made their last appearance together.

Joe made 2 appearances for the Football League and toured Australia with the Football Association, but his greatest achievement was to become one of the few central defenders who were a delight to watch, described by one former player and manager, as 'the greatest game reader I have ever seen', such was the timing and judgement of his interceptions.

His last first-team appearance was in February 1966 and then he coached the younger United players before taking, in October 1967, the position of manager with York City. He resigned in 1968 but became the manager of Chesterfield in 1973, remaining at Saltergate until 1976.

Jimmy Simmons
Forward, 1909-20

	Appearances	Goals
League	204	43
FA Cup	18	6
FL Cup	-	-
Other	79	18
TOTAL	301	67

Jimmy Simmons, United's outside right in the 1915 Cup Final, came from Blackwell, the same Derbyshire mining village as Bill Foulke, and he was a near relation of the great goalkeeper. Simmons joined United in November 1908 and made his first-team debut towards the end of that season.

Normally an inside right, though he could and did play on the left, he quickly settled into the team, proving to be both quick and clever and a prolific goal-scorer. In December 1912, United experimented by moving him to outside right, having already tried Joe Kitchen in that position, and although he wasn't happy there (nor was Kitchen), it was on the wing that he spent most of his time with United.

Described as a 'will o' the wisp', he had a big heart but was susceptible to injuries. He played a major part when United reached the FA Cup semi-final in 1914 but had the misfortune to be injured in the first few minutes of the big match. One year later, Simmons scored the first goal in United's comparatively easy victory against Chelsea in the Cup Final at Old Trafford, smashing a long centre from Utley, from a narrow angle, against the far post and into the net.

Simmons worked at Blackwell Colliery in the early part of the First World War, playing fairly regularly for United, before joining the Services at the beginning of 1918. He also made one appearance in September 1916 for Blackpool, reportedly while he was on his honeymoon.

Jimmy still showed some of his old brilliance when First Division football resumed after the war was over, but he missed much of the campaign due to injuries and United were happy to accept an offer from West Ham United of more than £1,000 for him. He had two seasons with the Hammers and later became a licensee in Matlock.

Ronnie Simpson
Outside left, 1958-64

	Appearances	Goals
League	203	44
FA Cup	26	2
FL Cup	7	1
Other	3	0
TOTAL	239	47

Ronnie Simpson was the United outside left in the team that was built by Joe Mercer and which finally achieved promotion in 1961. His nephew, Paul Simpson, played for United on loan from Wolverhampton Wanderers during the 1998/99 season.

Born in February 1934 in Carlisle, Simpson's pace and shooting power soon attracted attention and he joined Huddersfield Town. He made his League debut in October 1951 when he was seventeen, but it was not until 1956 that he claimed a regular first-team place, performing mainly at inside left. Joe Mercer, the United manager, tried to sign Simpson in 1957, but Bill Shankley, the Town manager, refused a bid of £10,000 – United were prepared to pay £15,000 – remarking that £20,000 wasn't enough. Six months later, however, in May 1958, he agreed a deal, by which Simpson joined United in exchange for Derek Hawksworth and about £6,000.

Ronnie had played mainly at inside left for Huddersfield and that was his position in his early days at the Lane, but he was soon moved to the left-wing role and grew to prefer it. With good pace and a strong left foot, he was an important member of the team that John Harris inherited from Mercer and which eventually won promotion to the former First Division and reached the FA Cup semi-final in 1961. His well-struck left-footed centres, taken at full stride on the run (which provided many of the opportunities that were turned into goals by Derek Pace), are the feature of his play that supporters will remember best.

Simpson would have been an even better player if he had been more forceful and, considering the power in his left foot, he should have scored more goals. He did, however, score one of United's quickest goals. It came after about eight seconds in a game at Burnley in October 1963 and, strangely enough, it was hit with the weak right foot.

Simpson spent six years at the Lane before joining Carlisle United for £4,950. He had the pleasure of being the only local player in the team which, later that season, won the Third Division championship trophy. Simpson later played for Queen of the South and then worked for Pearl Insurance and in the family retail business.

Jack Smith
Goalkeeper, 1930-49

	Appearances	Goals
League	347	0
FA Cup	31	0
FL Cup	-	-
Other	120	0
TOTAL	498	0

Jack Smith was an outstanding goalkeeper and a player remembered with genuine pleasure, whether by former colleagues, staff or supporters – not for nothing was he nicknamed 'Smiler'. His exemplary technique, his engaging smile and that dreadful old cap that he carried to each and every goalmouth (and occasionally wore), will be among the lasting memories of this fine 'keeper. That cap had once been new, but during Jack's playing days it looked as old as the man himself!

Born just to the north of Sheffield in September 1910, his family emigrated to Pittsburgh in the United States. Scenes that a boy in England might see on the cinema screen became real life, for he saw a man shot in the street just a few paces away and school meant baseball, basketball and American football. Like many other famous goalkeepers, he first took up the position because no other boy would volunteer to play in goal. Jack had introduced soccer to his school in Pittsburgh; the American boys loved the game and 'Smithy' was appointed coach – but he also had to be goalkeeper because the other boys thought it was a 'cissy job'.

His family returned to England when he was in his mid-teens and he played as an inside forward for Bolsterstone in the Penistone & District League. An injury to the goalkeeper led to him having a go between the posts and, this time, he decided to make it his position. He was spotted by Sheffield Wednesday and signed as an amateur, playing in their midweek team and gaining additional experience on Saturdays with Worksop Town.

Wednesday didn't show any further serious interest and he jumped at the chance of a 'trial' with United – for both Jack and his father supported the Blades. The 'trial' turned out to be a Central League match at Goodison Park. Everton fielded six internationals and won 4-0, but a second game brought an offer of terms. When he returned home with the news, Jack thought his father was going to kiss him, such was his enthusiasm.

His first-team debut came later that season and, from 1932 onwards, Smith was regarded as United's number one 'keeper, although he did face problems that threatened his career. There were injuries, particularly during the 1932/33 season and then, in the following season which ended in relegation, Smith suffered from 'a loss of confidence'. The reason became clear during the close season, when he decided that playing tennis would strengthen a wrist that had been troubling him. The 'cure' was a failure, and an investigation revealed that at

'All is safely gathered in.' Jack Smith shows how to do it against the background of the cricket pavilion. Fred Furniss is the other United player.

some time in the past, Jack had fractured his wrist – which had reset, but not in a correct fashion. That problem was solved and 'Smithy' became the very best of 'keepers.

Jack was about 5ft 10in tall and smart in both his appearance and in his work. He was very agile and looked (and was) confident and reliable with a sound technique – his catching of a high ball was well nigh perfect and he had no weaknesses (other than a superstition that he had to be the first player, after the captain, onto the field). He was cheerful, popular with other members of the team, and offered one hundred per cent reliability to the United defenders. He was very unlucky to miss out on international honours.

He played well in the 1936 Cup Final and had no chance of stopping Ted Drake's goal. He recalled seeing Drake's left foot going back as he prepared to shoot and, the next second, hearing the ball hit the back of the net. Happier memories were the promotion campaign in the 1938/39 season and, soon after the war had intervened, he had set a United record by appearing in 193 consecutive fixtures. He would later establish a further United record by playing in 203 consecutive League fixtures.

He served in the RAF during the war, playing as a guest player for Fulham, Sheffield Wednesday, Grimsby Town, Lincoln City, Everton, WBA and Manchester City, and had few opportunities to play for United before the 1944/45 season. He was a member of the 1945/46 League North Championship team and played regularly after the war until 1949.

It was thought that he had played for the last time when he was chaired from the field by his colleagues at the end of a County Cup match at Oakwell, but an injury crisis at the Lane brought him back for two further games in September 1949. He was a member of the training staff from 1949 until 1952, turning out for the reserves at the age of forty. He died in Sheffield in April 1986.

Mick Speight
Midfielder, 1971-80

	Appearances	Goals
League	199	14
FA Cup	9	1
FL Cup	8	1
Other	25	1
TOTAL	241	17

Michael Speight was one of the grittiest and most determined United players of the last thirty years and also read the game well. He was, however, let down by a lack of pace and he had the misfortune to spend the greater part of his time at the Lane in a period when the club was in serious decline.

Mick was born in Upton in November 1951. The son of a miner, he was a product of South Yorkshire football, playing for Don & Dearne Boys. He joined United when he was sixteen, but he didn't make his first-team debut until he was twenty, coming on as a last-minute substitute against West Ham United in November 1971. His full debut came in February 1972 and he began to hold a regular first-team place towards the end of 1973.

Partly because of injuries, he missed much of the 1975/76 season, when United were relegated, and virtually all of the following campaign. He took over the captaincy in the 1978/79 season, when United plunged into the old Third Division, and was transferred by Harry Haslam, the United manager, to Blackburn Rovers in July 1980 for a fee that was reported to be £40,000.

Speight was chosen for the England 'B' team that toured New Zealand, Malaysia and Singapore in 1978 and was a first-class professional, willing to play anywhere and offering total dedication, loyalty and a will to win. Strong and hard in the tackle, he was often given a specific 'marking' task, reducing the threat of a dangerous opponent and, if there were few frills to his play, he offered far more than being 'just a workhorse' – which were his words of self-description when he was a young man.

After leaving United, Speight spent two seasons at Ewood Park and a further couple with Grimsby Town, before he ended his League career with Chester City, where he acted, first as player-coach and then player-manager. He was quite successful, but too outspoken for the directors, and was replaced in the summer of 1986. In recent years, he has coached and managed various clubs in Norway.

Paul Stancliffe
Central defender, 1983-90

	Appearances	Goals
League	278	12
FA Cup	24	3
FL Cup	21	4
Other	18	1
TOTAL	341	20

All professional footballers bring their own qualities to the game, but when we speak of a player as a 'model professional' or 'true professional', then we are thinking of those special qualities that allow a manager to sleep peacefully at night and which we may describe as dedication, composure, loyalty and courage. Paul Stancliffe was clearly a true professional and his managers, colleagues and the supporters were well aware of the fact.

He was born in Sheffield in May 1958 and signed schoolboy forms for Sheffield Wednesday's manager, Danny Williams. Williams was sacked in 1971 and Paul eventually was released. Rotherham United took him under their wing and he made remarkable progress, making his first-team debut when he was sixteen and his League debut soon after his seventeenth birthday. He held that first-team place, playing 46 games in his first season.

He was a member of the Rotherham team that secured the Third Division championship in 1981, the Millers moving up as the Blades sank into the Fourth Division. Rotherham had a fine first season in the Second Division and Paul was unlucky not to be given representative honours. A bad tackle, in September 1982, took him out of the game for some months and was a prime cause of Rotherham returning to the Third Division. Paul was unsettled, asked for a transfer and was ready to join Barnsley, when Ian Porterfield, his former manager at Rotherham, stepped in and brought him to Bramall Lane.

The transfer forms were signed in July 1983 and the press reported that United had paid £100,000 for the big defender – but how much money actually moved between the clubs remains unclear. This became obvious when United's Mike Trusson moved to Millmoor as the year drew to a close, for the transfers were linked. In essence, 'Stan' was valued at about £100,000 and Trusson perhaps at £70,000.

'Stan' was an instant success with United and soon took over the captaincy. The season ended with a return to the Second Division, although United had a nail-biting finish, relying on Hull City failing to add a further goal to the two that they scored in their last game.

Off-the-field problems, which were not just a matter of a lack of money, formed an almost permanent background to the football scene at Bramall Lane during the 1980s, but through all that time, Stancliffe provided substance, stability and hope in the many periods of near despair (and some rather dire football). Players came and went and three – Phil Thompson, Lewington and Kuhl – were given the team

Four Stoke City defenders make it difficult for Paul, while United's Dean Glover offers some support.

captaincy, but in 1988 United found themselves back in the Third Division.

Dave Bassett had arrived and this new brush certainly cleaned. Little remained of the old when Bassett decided to create a team in his image, but Stancliffe was retained. Bassett knew integrity when it stared him in the face and 'Stan' led United straight back to the Second and on to the old First Division.

Paul was once quoted as saying, 'I've always played to my limitations'. Those are the words of a modest but intelligent man. He wasn't a Bobby Moore, but then he didn't pretend to be. He used the attributes he had and the skills he had worked on and did a job of work. He was tall (6ft 2in) and good in the air and he was strong and knew how to use his weight and resist a challenge. He had two good feet, read the game well and anticipated the moves of opponents. He covered well and marshalled his fellow defenders with know-how and authority, and his tackling was well-timed and determined. Above all else, he gave wholehearted commitment and his conduct, on and off the field, was a credit to the game.

Paul captained United on their return to the First Division, but Dave Bassett, wanting younger men at the heart of the defence, informed the player that he would be given a free transfer as a gesture to reward his loyal service to United. Paul returned to Millmoor on loan, and then received an offer of a contract from Wolves and moved there in December 1990.

He moved to York City in the close season of 1991 and his last season as a player was 1994/95. He had helped earlier with coaching and is now the head of youth development.

Albert Sturgess
Defender, 1908-23

	Appearances	Goals
League	353	5
FA Cup	22	0
FL Cup	-	-
Other	137	0
TOTAL	512	5

Albert Sturgess was never a 'brilliant' player, but he offered the qualities that all clubs and their managers seek and which all supporters recognize and admire. He was a diligent professional, and what you got from Sturgess was consistency, honesty and reliability. His tackling and anticipation were excellent and he was once described as a 'one-man football team', for he could and would play anywhere in the defence and he would also, in an emergency, play in goal if the goalkeeper was injured.

He was born in Etruria (Stoke-on-Trent) in October 1882 and joined the old Stoke Football Club around the turn of the century. They became bankrupt in 1908 and the players were offered for sale; Sturgess and a forward called Gallimore joined United for the princely sum of £50.

In appearance, he was 'all arms and legs', a strong, fearless player who 'never stopped'. Tall and slim, Sturgess, who was nicknamed 'Hairpin', stepped straight into the United first team and remained there. He suffered few injuries but, in any case, he would always play if at all possible, never wishing to lose his place and, for the same reason, he would play in any position given half a chance. At first he played as a half-back and, as he was two-footed, left, right or centre made not a jot of difference to him and he soon added full-back to his repertoire. All that mattered to Albert was that his name appeared on the team sheet.

He toured South Africa in 1910 with the FA, playing in 2 Test matches, and won 2 full international caps, playing at left half for England in 1911 and at right half in 1914. He played at right half in United's Cup Final victory in 1915 and had two spells as United's captain.

Sturgess may have expected to finish his playing career at the Lane, but in the close season of 1923 he was transferred to Norwich City, who needed to stiffen their defence. Sturgess was appointed captain of the Canaries and holds the record as the oldest player to make his debut for Norwich.

Albert retired from the game in 1925 and returned to Sheffield. He died there in July 1957.

Gerry Summers
Left-half, 1957-64

	Appearances	Goals
League	260	4
FA Cup	32	3
FL Cup	6	0
Other	7	0
TOTAL	305	7

When Joe Mercer signed Gerry Summers from West Bromwich Albion in May 1957, he had almost completed the building of a defence that would eventually take the Blades back to the top flight and provide the club and supporters with regular FA Cup victories (although a trip to Wembley remained a round too far).

Gerald Summers was born in October 1933 and brought up in the Small Heath district of Birmingham. He joined the West Bromwich Albion office staff and played for their junior teams. Although he was given a taste of reserve-team football when he was sixteen, it was not until December 1955 that he made his League debut. Summers was afraid that he had little chance of securing the regular left half spot in the Albion team, for it was held by the accomplished English international, Ray Barlow.

United paid £3,000 for Summers, which was a bargain. He made his debut at The Valley and, a little over a week later, Brian Richardson was given the right half position – what would be the most famous defensive formation in United's history was in place.

Gerry was a constructive midfield player and 'the brains of the side; a player of real perception, imagination and flair'. He played with determination, was quick to cover, had two good feet and provided an excellent link between defence and attack – always being available to take a pass from a fellow defender and move it forward with accuracy.

United had a fine team, though it was not until 1961 that promotion was eventually achieved. Their FA Cup record was excellent: they were very unlucky not to reach the semi-final stage in 1960, but did succeed in the following year and it was only a first-minute injury to Summers in 1962 which almost certainly robbed them of another semi-final place. The famous six defenders last played together in August 1963 and it was another rare injury in a Cup tie in 1964 that brought Gerry's first-team days with United to a close.

He was transferred in April 1964 to Hull City and moved to Walsall in October 1965, where he did some coaching: this aspect of the game had long been of interest to him and he was a FA qualified coach. He joined the Wolves coaching staff and then became an FA staff coach before accepting his first managerial position in July 1969 at Oxford United, who were then in the Second Division. He was sacked in October 1975, although it could be argued that he had done well to retain Oxford's Second Division status. He took over the reins at Gillingham, remaining there until 1981. In later years, he held coaching positions with Leicester City and Derby County.

Harry Thickett
Right-back, 1891 and 1893-1904

	Appearances	Goals
League	259	0
FA Cup	40	1
FL Cup	-	-
Other	11	0
TOTAL	310	1

Harry Thickett was one of the United heroes of the early days of the club, winning two England caps, a Football League Championship medal in 1898, two Cup Final winners medals in 1899 and 1902, and a runner-up medal in 1901. In his 299 League and Cup appearances for United, he never played in any other position than right-back.

Harry was born in Hexthorpe, near Doncaster, in 1873 and played five games for United early in 1891. He ended that season with Doncaster Rovers and then became a professional with Rotherham Town. United had obviously kept an eye on his progress and paid the Rotherham club £30 for his transfer in November 1893. He stepped straight into the first team and his form was so good that, three months later, he was selected to play for the Football League.

He was quite a big and sturdy man but surprisingly quick. His kicking was fine, but his outstanding qualities were willingness and hard work – perhaps best described by the word 'pluck' (which has now rather gone out of fashion). His honesty was exemplified when he offered to take a cut in wages in 1895 because he had missed so many games because of typhoid fever. He often played when he shouldn't have and this led to the oft-repeated tale that he had been injured prior to the 1899 Cup Final and had played swathed in forty yards of bandages and aided by copious amounts of whisky to kill the pain. The story had been fed to the press after the match by a Manchester doctor who specialized in treating injured players but, some days after the final, he said that he had spoken 'in jest'.

Thickett joined Bristol City in 1904 and then became the club's most successful manager, setting several club records in gaining promotion and then narrowly failing to win the old First Division championship in 1907 and reaching the FA Cup final in 1910. He later became a licensee in Trowbridge and died there in November 1920.

Simon Tracey
Goalkeeper, 1988-present

	Appearances	Goals
League	291	0
FA Cup	18	0
FL Cup	20	0
Other	11	0
TOTAL	340	0

Simon Tracey has made more first-team appearances for United than any other player since Len Badger, Tony Currie and Alan Woodward hung up their boots – and there would have been far more but for the competition he faced from Alan Kelly between 1992 and 1999.

Tracey was born in South London in 1967 and was sixteen when he joined Wimbledon and faced the problem of taking Dave Beasant's first-team place. Beasant was an excellent 'keeper and never missed a single game as Tracey waited for an opportunity. It eventually came when Beasant was transferred to Newcastle United soon after the Dons' FA Cup final victory and Tracey, as a consequence, made his debut in the Charity Shield match at Wembley when Liverpool gained some consolation for their FA Cup final defeat by winning 2-0. A week later, Simon conceded five goals in the first League match of the season.

Dave Bassett, the United manager in 1988, and a former Wimbledon manager, had not forgotten Tracey and brought him to Sheffield in October of that year for a fee of about £12,500. He made his debut in a Sherpa Van Trophy match at Wrexham and played in the final six League matches, when United secured promotion. He was an ever-present in the following season, when United returned to the First Division.

He missed the end of the 1991/92 season because of a shoulder injury and missed much of the following season with the same injury. By this time he had the pressure of competition from Alan Kelly. Kelly became an international and Tracey was also considered by Ireland, though it was felt that the Irish family link was not strong enough, and an injury robbed him of the opportunity of training with the English squad in 1992.

Tracey was in goal when United were relegated in 1994 and had the heartbreak of conceding the last-minute goal in the play-off final in 1997. Earlier, he had short spells on loan with Manchester City, Norwich City and Wimbledon but soldiered on, somewhat in Kelly's shadow, until the other 'Irishman' was transferred in the summer of 1999.

United's supporters continue to argue over the respective merits and failings of the two fine 'keepers. Both were athletic and capable of making great saves and their obvious errors were rare indeed. While Kelly may have dealt better with an onrushing forward, some would argue that Tracey's long kicking was more accurate and led to more 'route one' goals. In the end, United were fortunate to have had both.

Fred Tunstall
Outside left, 1920-33

	Appearances	Goals
League	437	129
FA Cup	35	5
FL Cup	-	-
Other	19	1
TOTAL	491	135

The player who scores the only goal in an FA Cup final is bound to be remembered, but Fred Tunstall could also be regarded as United's finest-ever wing forward. He certainly didn't look athletic and 'couldn't head a ball for toffee', but he had great speed and was particularly noted for the power of his shooting with both feet and for his fine, hard centres. He could pass his opponent on either side and it was said of him that no man hit a ball with more force and less apparent effort.

Tunstall was born in Newcastle-under-Lyme in Staffordshire in May 1897, but his family moved to Low Valley, Darfield, near Barnsley when he was a child. He worked as a miner at Houghton Main Colliery, near Barnsley, but had played little football until he joined the Royal Horse Artillery in 1915. Demobbed in January 1919, Tunstall was playing for Darfield St George when he first came to United's notice, but the scout sent to watch him was not impressed. Barnsley also turned him down, but in August 1920 he joined Scunthorpe United. His potential ability rapidly became obvious and, in December, after only nineteen games for the Lincolnshire club, United paid a record fee for a non-League player of £1,000 for his transfer. There was little publicity for the move and, as a result, at the very moment that Tunstall was making his debut for the Blades at White Hart Lane, Peter McWilliam, the Spurs manager, was taking his seat at Scunthorpe, hoping to watch this brilliant new prospect.

Tunstall played regularly for United for the next ten years, rarely missing a game, and he was fortunate in that, for virtually all of that time, his partner at inside left in the United team was Billy Gillespie, the Irish international captain, and that George Green, an English international, played behind him at left half.

Tunstall was fast and strong with a long raking stride. He was an advocate of first-time shooting and centres – both were usually struck with awesome power. Harry Johnson, United's record scoring centre forward, certainly profited from Fred Tunstall's fine crosses and said that 'you would think twice about putting your head to them' – although Harry was usually the first on the spot to score when one of Tunstall's powerful shots was not gathered by the goalkeeper. Jimmy Dunne, the Irish international who took Johnson's place in the Blades' forward line, scored so often from a Tunstall centre that 'Tunny-Dunnit' became a staple headline in the Sheffield newspapers. Tunstall also had a fine record from the penalty spot,

Fred's caps and medals were featured on this postcard.

although he did miss two in one game against Notts County.

Fred was awarded 7 England international caps. He missed the 1925 FA tour of Australia because the tour party left before the Cup Final, but he toured Canada in 1926 and also played for the Football League.

His most famous goal came after 31 minutes of play in the 1925 FA Cup final. A long crossfield ball from the Sheffield right fell just outside the corner of the penalty area. Wake, the Cardiff City right half-back 'was the only player in the vicinity. Tunstall was coming up a dozen yards away. The half-back saw the forward's approach but allowed the ball to roll on, intending possibly to feint and secure a more helpful clearance up the Cardiff right wing.' There seemed enough time for the manoeuvre, but he had waited one second too long. 'Wake caught napping' became the inevitable headline. 'Tunstall charged up, took the ball off his toe, and had a clear course for goal. He moved forward a few strides and shot the ball a foot or so inside the far post'. Unresolved are the questions as to who crossed the ball and which foot Fred used to score? As to the goal, most of the team said the left foot but Milton and Sampy – who was the unlucky twelfth man – and Fred's wife said the right and Tunstall, in those circumstances, was happy enough to agree with his spouse.

Tunstall was transferred to Halifax Town in February 1933 for £400, but later became a legendary figure with Boston, serving them for over thirty years as a player, manager, coach, trainer and groundsman. He died there in July 1971.

George Utley
Left half, 1913-22

	Appearances	Goals
League	107	4
FA Cup	15	5
FL Cup	-	-
Other	118	15
TOTAL	240	24

In Sheffield United's early days, the club were fortunate to find two great captains. The first was Billy Hendry, who laid the foundations for the early success of the club, and the second was Ernest Needham, who led United during 'golden years' of success. United's third great captain was George Utley.

Before the 1920s, the captain of a football team was in almost total command of the tactics and formation of the team once a match had commenced and his position and significance within the club was far more important than today. From about 1905, United had gone through a comparatively barren period and their FA Cup record had been particularly poor. By 1912, there was a growing feeling within the club that a new captain might be the key to a return to days of fame and fortune and United decided that George Utley, the Barnsley right half (and still the only Barnsley player to win a full England cap), would be the best man to provide the necessary leadership and inspiration that the team required.

Utley was born in Elsecar, near Barnsley, in May 1887 and had a trial with the Wednesday, but he was injured and heard nothing more from them. He joined Barnsley in 1908 and played an important role when Barnsley reached the Cup Final in 1910. Barnsley's success in winning the trophy in 1912, in the replayed final at Bramall Lane, only served to add to United's misery, for their recent record in the competition had been so poor.

Utley was a big, bustling, strong midfield player with the longest throw of his time – though Ernest Milton once remarked that George threw with one hand but got away with it. Utley could play up front and 'was a good dribbler for a big man' and he was blessed with a hard shot. He had driving inspirational qualities: he was a fighter, always determined to win and he used his weight to effect on the field at a time when charging was more part and parcel of the game (though he felt that referees often penalised him unfairly). He also played with intelligence and, using his powers as captain, would seek to dictate the pattern of play.

United signed Utley in November 1913 and had to pay £2.000 for his transfer – that equalled the record fee at the time – and in order to persuade him to move, United had to offer him a five-year contract and the promise of a future benefit. Those decisions were to provide United with problems in the future, but the Blades would never regret signing the big man from Elsecar. Under his leadership, United reached the semi-final stage of the FA

The 1915 FA Cup-winning team.

Cup in his first season (losing 1-0 to Burnley in a replay) and won the trophy twelve months later. Utley scored a magnificent goal in the 1915 semi-final and led the team to victory in the final against Chelsea, United dominating the game throughout and winning 3-0. Utley, according to George Waller, the United trainer and coach, was 'a tower of strength, particularly in a cup-tie, and a clever leader of men.'

When First Division football resumed in 1919, Utley was thirty-two, but the agreement regarding future benefits remained unfilled. The contract concerned the player receiving the net receipts from a League match, but there were other United players (who had given longer service than Utley) who felt no less deserving than the captain. Matters came to a head in February 1920. Utley chose the fixture against Sunderland but secured a minimum guarantee of £500. Gillespie, Cook, Fazackerley and Gough accepted the same figure, but Utley was fortunate in that the net receipts from the Sunderland match brought him more than twice that amount.

By 1921, Utley was no longer an automatic first-team player and he was transferred to Manchester City in September 1922. A little over a year later, he took the position of trainer and coach with Bristol City and, after a year at Ashton Gate and a further year at Hillsborough, he moved to Fulham, before leaving the game in 1928. George had taken over George Waller's sports shop in Bramall Lane but now moved to the Fylde district of Lancashire, where he did some coaching at Rossall School – he had played cricket as well as football for United. He died in Blackpool in January 1966. Mementos of Utley's great career now feature in United's Hall of Fame.

Dane Whitehouse
Left side attacker/defender, 1988-97

	Appearances	Goals
League	231	38
FA Cup	17	2
FL Cup	21	8
Other	9	3
TOTAL	278	51

We all share the tragedy when the career of a fine player is cut short through injury and it was a bitter blow for the player, club and supporters when it happened to Dane Whitehouse, for he was an extremely good player who was beginning to play with even greater confidence and quality.

Whitehouse was born in Sheffield in October 1970 and signed schoolboy forms for the Blades when he was fourteen. He made his first-team debut at Blackpool the day after his eighteenth birthday and after only six full appearances with the reserve team. Dane was playing on the left wing but had strength and could tackle and Dave Bassett, the United manager, also occasionally played him in a more withdrawn left-side position in midfield or at left-back.

He became a regular first-team player in the 1991/92 season, but there was strong competition from Glyn Hodges and Roger Nilsen for a permanent place on the left flank of the United team and he had the misfortune, in October 1992, to suffer a broken shin. He returned to the team, playing in a more defensive role against Blackburn in the FA Cup sixth round tie and then against Wednesday in the 1993 semi-final tie at Wembley, but soon returned to a more attacking left-side midfield role for which he was ideally suited.

He was a consistent and reliable player with a 'good engine'. He could attack and defend and was equipped with a good touch and a strong shot with his left foot. He was also skilful and could go past an opponent and put in a dangerous centre, besides being particularly lethal in meeting crosses from the right wing. He had an excellent record with penalty kicks.

His fine career came to an end as a result of a dreadful tackle at Port Vale in November 1997. After a year of rehabilitation and two knee operations, Dane attempted a comeback in pre-season friendly matches and reserve-team fixtures, but it was to no avail and his playing career was over. A benefit match was played at the Lane in May 2001, when Whitehouse delighted his supporters by scoring a hat-trick.

Mick Whitham
Defender, 1890-97

	Appearances	Goals
League	86	1
FA Cup	17	0
FL Cup	-	-
Other	57	0
TOTAL	160	1

Mick Whitham serves as a reminder of United's incredible progress in their first ten seasons. He played in the club's first season and, by the time he was transferred in 1899, United had won the League Championship and FA Cup. Whitham also shares, with Harry Lilley, the honour of being United's first international. This was in March 1892, when United were playing in the Northern League. Whitham played against Ireland and Lilley against Wales, but both matches were played on the same day!

Whitham was born in Ecclesfield in November 1867 and was a file-cutter by trade. In his younger days, he was a fast and robust midfield player, turning out for several clubs, including Thorpe Hesley, Ecclesfield, the Wednesday, Lockwood Brothers and Rotherham Swifts. By the time he joined United in 1890, he was usually playing fullback, though he was equally at home in any of the half-back positions.

Whitham and Rab Howell had both been playing for Rotherham Swifts when they were given a trial with United in March 1890. United were well aware that they needed far better players if football was to be a success at the Lane and capturing two future internationals in one day was certainly a step in the right direction. Whitham played in the club's first competitive fixture in the Midland Counties League and then in the Northern and the Football League. He played in the test match which took United into the old First Division and he played in the first game at that level. He also had the satisfaction of making an appearance in the 1897/98 season, when the League Championship was won.

Mick was as 'strong as a horse' and came to United with a 'reputation for roughness'. This author has seen him described as 'one of the most vigorous chargers Sheffield has ever had' (in a period when charging was part and parcel of the game). He wasn't usually too popular with the opposition supporters and, after one particularly rough encounter at Middlesbrough, he had them baying for blood and threatening violence. The players had changed at a pub some distance from the ground and the walk back passed by a duck pond and it was there that Mick took his stand, rolled up his sleeves and issued an invitation to the 'best man in Middlesbrough to step forward' – not surprisingly, there were no takers.

When his playing days were over he became a trainer with Rotherham Town, Gainsborough Trinity, Huddersfield Town and Brentford and it was while he was with the West London club that he died in May 1924.

Bernard Wilkinson
Centre half, 1900-13

	Appearances	Goals
League	373	14
FA Cup	23	0
FL Cup	-	-
Other	1	0
TOTAL	397	14

Sheffield United's cricket and football followers often referred to Bernard Wilkinson as a 'pocket Hercules'. He was certainly small in stature, but he was a bundle of energy as a centre half and a mighty hitter on the cricket field. An international and yet a part-timer at football, he rejected, because of his work, the opportunity to play cricket for Yorkshire.

Bernard was born in September 1879 and was a native of Thorpe Hesley, a village to the east of Sheffield. He joined United as a nineteen-year-old part-time professional in 1899 and made his first-team debut in March of the following year. He secured a regular first-team place in the autumn of 1901 and, by the end of that season, was the proud holder of a FA Cup medal. Two years later he played for England against Scotland at Hampden but, though England were successful, he was never selected again.

Bernard was only 5ft 6in tall; indeed the tale was told that he was once refused entry at the Meadow Lane players' entrance as 'they don't have little 'uns like you playing football.' All men and women were much smaller in those days, however, and centre halves were genuine half-backs rather than defenders – those of you who remember Joe Shaw will not need reminding that a great centre half does not have to be tall. Wilkinson was a different type of player to Shaw, however, being 'thick set' with 'broad shoulders' and relying more on speed, formidable strength and tackling. He was famed for long, sweeping passes to the wing but his shooting was poor, the end product normally sailing over the bar.

A part-time player, Wilkinson was a cheerful, energetic character employed in the fish and poultry trade. An all-round sportsman, he was offered a contract by the Yorkshire County Cricket Club but turned it down because of his work. His brother, Billy, however, was a Yorkshire player and a United footballer but he didn't have the charisma in either sport of Bernard. Bernard was satisfied to play cricket as a professional for United, where his furious batting made him a great favourite with the spectators as he regularly dispatched the ball into Bramall Lane.

Bernard took over the United captaincy during the 1909/10 season, but the old days of glory had gone and, in January 1912, he resigned the captaincy and was given a free transfer. He joined Rotherham Town and played with them until the outbreak of the First World War in August 1914. He died in Sheffield in May 1949.

Alan Woodward
Outside right, 1964-78

	Appearances	Goals
League	538	158
FA Cup	25	3
FL Cup	32	14
Other	48	18
TOTAL	643	193

Alan Woodward was an outside right of the very highest quality and a quite thrilling player to watch – and yet his list of achievements in the game from the viewpoint of honours, caps and medals was slim. He was fast and clever, two footed with a powerful shot and his pinpoint crosses were devastating weapons. His corner kicks were a delight and provided a threat to opponents that none could solve. They were struck with marvellous precision, very hard, and with just the right weight and height. Some were straight and others, delivered with the outside of the right boot, came with a vicious swerve. However, one was always aware that there was something lacking and that prevented him from achieving the highest awards in the game.

Woodward was born in September 1946 and brought up in Silkstone Common, near Barnsley. He played for Barnsley boys when they won the English Schools Shield competition in 1961 and became a United apprentice in April 1962. He was one of the splendid group of essentially local youngsters that played in the early 1960s in the Northern Intermediate League side and then in the old First Division. Alan made his League debut at Anfield in October 1964 and held his place.

United were relegated in 1968, but developed an exciting attacking style that provided 'Woody' with plenty of scope that he exploited to the full, attacking defenders on either side with speed and directness and cutting in to finish with awesome power. He was the leading United scorer in the League that season and in the next two, scoring 18 League goals in the 1969/70 campaign and 15 when promotion was secured in the next and there were four other seasons when he led the United list of scorers in the League. Particularly memorable moments were his first hat-trick, which came in 1970 at Fratton Park, and the four goals against Ipswich Town in November 1971. Another hat trick followed in 1973 against Southampton.

Alan had other strings to his bow. He was a very capable deputy goalkeeper and performed particularly well in the challenging game against Leeds United in 1967, when he defied the opposition for eighty minutes. His record from the penalty spot was a good one, with only three failures in twenty-three attempts in the major League and Cup competitions.

Woodward was an England youth international and he was later to play for the Football League, but a full international cap never came his way. It was, of course, the era of Alf Ramsey's 'wingless wonders', when the num-

A typical smash hit from 'Woody' against Southampton in December 1973, when he recorded a hat trick. Geoff Salmons and Keith Eddy look on.

ber seven England shirt was worn by players of a different style, such as Alan Ball or Francis Lee. Alan never had the opportunity which he deserved. He might have seized it, but I doubt it. His failing was said to be lack of self belief. John Harris, United's manager, said of him that he only had one fault. 'He simply has no conception of how much talent he has.' This lack of confidence was obvious at an early age. If he made an early error, his play suffered but, if a goal came his way, he was a totally different player. Such is confidence. Sadly for football managers, it has always been so and Alan was also one of those players who would frequently play better after a half-time roasting from John Harris. Perhaps he was not a player for the really big occasion; he – and United at that time – rarely shone in the FA Cup but he was a wonderful player to watch.

Every fan of those days will have a favourite 'Woody' goal to remember and it was no surprise that he was the United's Player of the Year on three occasions. Only Joe Shaw and Alan Hodgkinson made more appearances for the Blades and only Harry Johnson scored more goals.

Alan captained the side in 1976 but, because of domestic problems, he moved to the United States in September 1978. He played for Tulsa Roughnecks for three seasons and then had a season of 'grid-iron' football as a goal kicker with the Oklahoma Thunder which, on occasions, drew him into action for just two minutes. He has also coached in the States, ran a sports store and worked for American Airlines. He still lives in Tulsa.